GOD

OF

SPERM

GOD
OF
SPERM

Cappy Rothman's Life in Conception
Joe Donnelly
with Cappy Rothman

RARE BIRD
LOS ANGELES, CALIF.

RARE BIRD

THIS IS A GENUINE RARE BIRD BOOK

Rare Bird Books
6044 North Figueroa Street
Los Angeles, California 90042
rarebirdbooks.com

For more information, address:
Rare Bird Books Subsidiary Rights Department
6044 North Figueroa Street
Los Angeles, California 90042

Inside Front Cover Photograph: Shaquille O'Neal and Cappy Rothman
Inside Back Cover Photograph: Cappy Rothman in his office, 1982

Set in Minion
Printed in the United States

10 9 8 7 6 5 4 3 2 1

Publisher's Cataloging-in-Publication Data available upon request.

Contents

Author's Note

At the summit of Mount Whitney, you have little choice but to focus on your breath because the altitude can take it away as surely as the scenery will. Topping out at 14,505 feet (and still growing), Mount Whitney is the highest point in the contiguous United States. In his younger days, Dr. Cappy Rothman made the summit three times, each time looking out at a world of expanding personal and professional horizons.

Cappy Miles Rothman has long appreciated the magnitude of nature and the multitudes it contains. For nearly a decade beginning in the mid-seventies, every August 12, he undertook a twenty-four-hour pilgrimage from his Pacific Palisades home to sleep under the stars on top of Yosemite National Park's Half Dome. Every summer, he'd leave in the morning, climb in the afternoon, be at the summit by dark to watch the Perseids meteor shower, before descending the next morning. Looking at the cosmic fireworks, Cappy would ponder the infinite possibilities

of the universe, the marvels of creation. He couldn't help but see parallels in the Yosemite night sky with the wonders of the body's inner space, particularly within the male reproductive system, which he'd begun studying in earnest during his medical residencies. Both contained billions of possibilities for generating life.

On top of Half Dome, Cappy must certainly have reflected on the time when a powerful US senator asked him to preserve his deceased son's reproductive capacity, and on how he would later change the meaning of "life after death" by playing a critical role in the birth of Brandalynn Vernoff, the first baby conceived of sperm retrieved from a clinically dead man.

Rothman had already started what would become the California Cryobank by then. Arguably the world's largest repository of human genetic material, the Cryobank is responsible for the conception of more than 230,000 individuals and counting. Soon enough, the number of humans who can trace their genetic legacy back to the California Cryobank may number in the millions. Its storage tanks hold enough frozen genetic material to repopulate a post-apocalyptic world, should such a time come. No surprise, Cappy Rothman is sometimes referred to as "the God of Sperm."

What is surprising, perhaps, is that this is also the legacy of the son of a notorious gangster—a child who spent his formative years around colorful Mob figures during Miami Beach's *Magic City*-era, a boy who shook Fulgencio Batista's hand, and a young man who partied in Havana with the sons of Batista's closest associates.

By the time Cappy started coming of age, his father, Norman Rothman, an erstwhile laborer and union man, had become Norman "Roughhouse" Rothman, a Mafia figure of growing interest to law enforcement and the FBI. Roughhouse cut a wide swath through the Mob's infamous mid-century expansions into Miami, Havana, and Las Vegas. He would be linked, with varying degrees of veracity, to such notable figures as Meyer Lansky, Santo Trafficante Jr., Fulgencio Batista, and Jack Ruby.

The son of Norman "Roughhouse" Rothman could have become any number of things. Those who knew Cappy as a well-connected bon vivant in velvet pants with a twenty-carat smile, a cool car, and carte blanche at the top hotspots (Was Sinatra playing at the Fontainebleau that night?) wouldn't have been surprised if he had maintained a certain momentum toward a life as a South Beach impresario, hotelier, or nightclub owner running a glamorous Cuban revue. A more whimsical possibility, given his childhood penchant for adopting castaway exotic pets, would have seen him opening a sanctuary for rescued animals on the edge of the Everglades.

So whatever Cappy Rothman might have done with his life, even his closest family and friends from back in the day would likely not have predicted that he'd become a groundbreaking doctor and controversial pioneer in the still-unfolding realms of male infertility, advanced reproductive technology, and an entirely new field of medicine called andrology. Rothman has likened his own contributions to "lighting a candle in a cave."

This book, the story of a remarkable American life and one man's profound impact on how we have children, is the product of much research, many interviews, and some helpful feedback—not to mention a successful Freedom of Information Act request to obtain the FBI files on Norman Rothman. Mostly, though, it's a product of the many days Cappy hosted me at his lovely late-modern home in Pacific Palisades, high up a winding canyon in the Santa Monica Mountains. The house was a risk when he bought it—after years of internships and residencies, Cappy's medical practice was just starting to take hold—but it felt very much like a piece of the American and Californian dreams Cappy had embraced.

We'd meet there in the afternoons, often in the backyard with a view over-looking the Pacific, talking either on the patio or under the gazebo next to the koi pond. More often than not, hummingbirds and bees buzzed around the garden while a sea breeze kept things cool. Inside, the house was tastefully decorated with Peter Beard and David Hockney originals, contemporary art, sculptures, keepsakes, and memorabilia Cappy and Beth, his wife of fifty-four years, have collected during their travels to more than seventy-seven countries around the world. The house reflects the confidence of self-made success without betraying any of the chest-puffing gaudiness that seems to accompany such things these days.

During these sessions, Rothman—tall, slim, garrulous, and mostly delighted with the way his unexpected life had turned out—told me of his metamorphosis from a scion of Roughhouse Rothman's underworld enterprises to a man in the middle of dramatic changes, not just in the way we reproduce, but also in the way we think of the biology, ethics, and metaphysics of reproduction.

Parenthood is now possible for infertile couples, same-sex couples, single women, transgender women. In theory, a child can now be born to a couple from an embryo conceived of gametes culled from donor eggs and donor sperm, making it a four-person project. If a surrogate is called upon to carry the embryo, that would make five. Advances in reproductive medicine have, in fact, made it possible for just about anybody to have a baby.

Some say this is well and good and represents a democratization of reproductive possibilities that opens up pathways to parenthood for millions who otherwise would have been denied that opportunity. Others say we're on the path toward the sort of commodification of reproduction that gets us one step closer to designer babies for the wealthy and mongrels for the rest. Whatever you may think of the ethical questions involving advanced reproductive medicine, or even if you think there are none, it's clear that science has been boldly exploring the final frontiers of human creation.

Cappy Rothman has been one of the captains on that ship ever since he set sail from Miami Beach to the Naval Hospital Corps School in Great Lakes, Illinois, where his journey of discovery and self-determination took off in earnest. As such, he will signify different things to different people—innovator, iconoclast, hero to many, villain to some. To me, he came to embody the postwar American landscape, a time and place of expanding horizons and infinite possibilities. It's hard to imagine his story taking place anywhere else.

What a journey.

—Joe Donnelly

Chapter 1

Life After Death

CAPPY ROTHMAN WAS AND is a huge *Star Trek* fan. The shelves in his home office are lined with collectibles— the Enterprise, Captain Kirk, "Bones" McCoy, Lieutenant Uhura. It probably won't surprise you that Rothman's favorite, and perhaps his biggest cultural hero, is Mr. Spock. "I like his character," says Cappy. "He's logical."

It's understandable that someone like Rothman, a futurist and a man of science, would appreciate Spock's preference for logic over emotion. But let's not forget that Spock was half human, and much to the chagrin of his Vulcan side, he too was occasionally swayed by emotion. "I think I'm the same," says Rothman. "I happen to be very sensitive…but I do like his logic."

Throughout his life, Rothman has taken Spock's signature saying, "Live long and prosper," to heart. He is, after all, a doctor whose enduring interest has been in the field of infertility, especially in the underappreciated (until relatively recently) male side of the conception equation: sperm.

Somewhere in the middle of this story, around the time major advances in reproductive medicine were igniting panic in some and a mixture of joy and relief in others, the possibility of turning Spock's salutation upside down landed at Rothman's door. The question it posed: Can you prosper even if you don't live long?

It started when the chief resident of neurosurgery at the UCLA Medical Center (now the Ronald Reagan UCLA Medical Center) called Rothman on behalf of then California Senator Alan Cranston. "Hey, Doc," the chief resident said to Cappy, "I've got this weird question from a senator who would like you to retrieve the sperm from his son…can you?"

The request was even weirder than it sounds. It came in the spring of 1980. By then, Rothman was several years down the road that would lead to him being known as "The God of Sperm," and the sperm bank Rothman had started in a utility closet half a decade earlier—the California Cryobank—was on its way to becoming one of the largest repositories of genetic material on the planet. So, collecting and storing sperm was not an issue. Not usually; this case was a little more complicated. The senator's first-born son—Robin, age thirty-two—had been in an accident on May 10 and was in a persistent vegetative state. The accident was a troubling coda to a troubled life. Robin had been arrested the year before the accident, charged with allegedly assaulting a former girlfriend and attempted arson at her Burbank home. Robin was unmarried and without children when a van struck him as he was getting into his car outside his home, causing the fatal head injuries that would have ruled out continued or future life.

The accident happened just shy of two years after Louise Joy Brown, the first "test-tube baby," arrived on the world stage, bringing to mind another of Rothman's favorite cultural references: Aldous Huxley's *Brave New World*. The 1932 sci-fi classic predicts a future in which technological advances in reproduction, entertainment, and psychological control are used to establish a complacent citizenry, lacking any creative energy or sense of the transcendent. It's an oddly dystopian choice for an optimist such as Rothman—perhaps the yin to his *Star Trek*–loving yang.

Regardless, when Louise Joy Brown made her debut in the summer of 1978—first on the cover of *Time* magazine in illustrated form as an orangey circle in a pink-liquid-filled test tube, and then to the entire world as a human baby—many thought Huxley's darker visions were coming true.

Senator Cranston knew of Patrick Steptoe and Robert Edwards, the gynecologist and embryologist who developed IVF and oversaw Louise Joy Brown's birth. He was aware of the possibilities of IVF and also of the ability to freeze and store sperm.

The senator was no stranger to hard times. His first wife, and mother of his two sons, had suffered a stroke, and the couple divorced a few years prior to Louise Joy Brown's birth. Now, here he was, sixty-six, with no grandchildren and about to lose one of his two sons. The senator didn't believe in miracles; he understood science. The caprices of life and death and the new world of reproductive possibilities tangoed in the heart and mind of the senator as he sat at the hospital next to his clinically dead son.

Ultimately, Senator Cranston reasoned that his childless son's genes didn't have to die with him. If Louise Joy Brown's birth had expanded the Overton window wide in the arena of reproduction, what Senator Cranston was proposing threatened to blow it wide open.

Now, with the chief resident on the phone, Cappy had to ponder whether to add more fuel onto the fire of ethical debates regarding the limits of conception—or rather the increasing lack of them. As preposterous as Senator Cranston's inquiry may seem to an outsider, Rothman, a fertility specialist, was intimate with people's desires to seek different outcomes than capricious fate seemed to have in store.

He went to the UCLA Medical Center to see the patient and his father. The senator asked how much the procedure might cost. "I said, 'Right now, nothing.' I wasn't even sure it could be done," says Rothman. "We didn't have computers or the internet. You couldn't Google anything. It was just a matter of what you could predict from what you knew."

After assessing the situation, Cappy called the chief resident at UCLA back and told him they had three options. One would be an intrathecal (spinal) injection of neostigmine—a drug that can cause the body to go into spasms. The thinking was that if the entire body could go into spasms, it might also ejaculate locally. With a catheter in place, the ejaculate could be recovered. Another option was to manually stimulate the patient, who was brain dead but still had functioning nerves and could conceivably achieve orgasm. The third way was to remove all the anatomy that could contain sperm—the entire male reproductive system—and attempt to harvest viable sperm.

After Cappy detailed the three options, he says the chief resident went silent.

"'Hey, Doc,' he said at last, breaking the silence with some gallows humor. 'I've been a neurosurgical resident for more than a year, and I can't tell you what I've been asked to do, but if you think I'm going to jerk off a dead man, you're crazy.'

"Okay," Cappy deadpanned. "Then, we have two options.'"

On May 16, following six days of unconsciousness, Robin Cranston was pronounced dead at 5:20 p.m. Cappy went to the hospital where he met briefly with Senator Cranston, a modest-looking man with presidential ambitions whom Cappy says had a presence about him, even in the middle of this harrowing ordeal.

"I was impressed by him and excited by what I was about to embark on, excited and looking forward to the opportunity," recalls Rothman.

Rothman decided the best approach would be to remove the reproductive anatomy and attempt to retrieve any viable sperm that was still stuck in the plumbing, so to speak. The senator's son was an organ donor, so Cappy had to wait for other organs to be harvested before he could get to the reproductive system. "By the time they said, 'Okay,' there was very little of the body left."

The room emptied, and Cappy was left there with the remains of the senator's son and the task of salvaging something profound from the tragedy: Robin's genes.

"I was there with myself and my instruments and good lighting, and I almost felt like Da Vinci in the 1400s... just dissecting in an operating room all alone, which was a wonderful opportunity...an education beyond what I already had in gross anatomy."

Cappy set about removing the testicles, the seminal vesicles (the glands that produce the semen that mixes with sperm during ejaculation), the vas deferens, and the epididymis—the twenty-foot "barrel of the gun" that is compressed into two inches of space and through which sperm travel over the span of several weeks in order to reach the vas deferens, where it remains poised for ejaculation. If the whole process sounds slow and ineffective, that's probably a matter of perspective. A sperm is microscopic and the distances it travels are great. For example, Rothman explains, the distance and time it takes for a sperm cell to travel from the cervix to the egg is analogous to a man running forty-four marathons in forty-five minutes.

If trying to perform a minor miracle of sorts for a powerful senator wasn't fraught enough, the fact that nobody had done this procedure before only added to the pressure. It was groundbreaking by definition. When Rothman made his first incursions into the dead man's reproductive system, he found no viable sperm in the vas deferens, which is the channel or duct where sperm waits to be ejaculated after it has traveled from the epididymis. There were no viable sperm to be seen in the seminal vesicle either.

This was as Cappy expected, though he was still relieved by this because even though these would be the obvious places to look for viable sperm, they are harder to reach than the epididymis, where sperm mature after being created in the testicles before heading on their way. Rothman found a significant amount of sperm lingering in the epididymis. He harvested some samples and after analyzing it, determined many of the sperm cells were still motile and viable. Less expected, he discovered that the testes themselves, where sperm is initially generated and not as likely to have reached maturity, also contained viable cells, though fewer in number.

The epididymis and the testicles were hiding viable sperm in plain sight. Rothman's research on human anatomy and on how sperm reaches its destination had given him a hunch. "I was not surprised. I had some awareness of what I would find based on my studies. I thought I would find sperm where I found it, and they were, in fact, viable," says Cappy.

The potentially more significant result of Rothman's extraordinary procedure was the discovery of how accessible viable sperm actually were. "When I found millions of sperm, it was an exciting discovery," explains Cappy. "It was a 'wow!' moment…One doesn't have to take the entire male reproductive system. One can take the epididymis and the testicular tissue and find sufficient sperm."

Rothman was able to aspirate enough fluid to freeze and store millions of Robin Cranston's motile sperm. This was a monumental and transgressive moment, outside of medical norms. There simply was no precedent with humans, and therefore, no ethical guidelines. "I couldn't think of a case of postmortem sperm retrieval," says Cappy. "I discovered an ethical case for postmortem sperm retrieval."

For Rothman, the abiding question wasn't so much a matter of whether he would do it, but if and how he could do it. Characteristically, he followed his own compass. "I would do almost anything if a patient wanted it done," he explains. "I was happy to go back and tell the senator that I found viable sperm."

The senator simply thanked Rothman, and the two never spoke again.

Senator Cranston never did anything with his son's sperm (a deferral that would prove to be typical over time in cases of postmortem sperm retrieval). Nonetheless, Rothman had sealed his place in medical history as the first person to retrieve viable reproductive cells from a clinically dead person. "It was unheard of," says Cappy, who was not only aware of the cutting edge but *was* the cutting edge.

The implications for male-factor infertility among the living were also enormous. Men whose sperm tested as subfertile in ejaculate might have viable sperm hiding somewhere along the sperm's long road from the testicles to the outside world. Perhaps, someday such latent sperm could be retrieved and used in advanced insemination procedures.

Just months after he performed the procedure on Cranston, Rothman published the groundbreaking, "A Method for Obtaining Viable Sperm in a Postmortem State," in the November 1980 edition of the American Fertility Society's *Fertility and Sterility* journal.

Though the article would help establish a standard operating procedure (one that is, by and large, still followed), it also sparked the expected furor over whether getting sperm from a dead person is a good idea.

"After this article was published, it became an ethical issue—should it be done?" says Cappy.

The ethical questions revolved around questions of consent, implied consent, parental legacy, inheritance issues, precedence, and more. The debates are still among the least settled in the field, partly because it's still such a rare request and procedure. Cappy didn't see a conflict in the Cranston case or with the family that subsequently called him to Riverside when their teenage son suffered a mortal gunshot wound, or later, when he played a key role in the first pregnancy and birth achieved with sperm retrieved from a clinically dead person. His job as a doctor, he says, was to relieve pain and suffering. He hasn't strayed from that perspective in the years since.

Fortuitously, the first case of postmortem sperm retrieval was also about as straightforward as something of this nature could be, and therefore a good candidate for the first attempt.

There was no family feud to navigate. The UCLA Medical Center was onboard, and the fact that the patient was an organ donor could be construed to imply consent. While the ethical debates over postmortem sperm retrieval would rage on for decades in its wake, the very first one was as tidy as could be when it comes to extracting genetic material from a dead man.

∼

IT WAS THE SAME Spock-like approach to the questions of life and death—or, if you will, the question of life after death—that propelled Cappy to jump into his beat-up Pontiac and drive into the sweltering depths of Riverside, California, on a summer day in 1982, just two years after his first experience with postmortem sperm retrieval.

By this time, Rothman was at a point in his life and career when he could have been driving a BMW or a Porsche. His medical practice had taken hold after a whirlwind of internships and residencies that had swept him through Parkland Memorial Hospital in Dallas, Harbor General in Torrance, UCSF Medical Center in San Francisco, and finally to Loma Linda Hospital, located in the city of Loma Linda in Southern California. There, after scoring ninety-seven percent on his urology board certification tests, Rothman had become a resident physician with a rising reputation under the guidance of Roger Barnes, the man who innovated the trans-urethral resection of the prostrate (TURP), which became the medical standard for urologists performing prostate resection surgery for benign enlarged prostates.

As for Riverside, it is a dusty Southern California exurb that's on few people's must-see lists, especially in the summer. Summer in Riverside is like summer in Las Vegas, only with more pollution and fewer attractions. Suffice it to say, there aren't many good reasons to venture there from coastal Los Angeles on a hot, summer day.

As it happened, Rothman had a good one: a call from Riverside Memorial Hospital. The family of a sixteen-year-old boy who was in a vegetative state following a gunshot wound wanted to know if anything could be done to preserve his legacy. He was the only son of a prominent Chinese family. His sperm needed to be extracted and put on ice immediately. As with Robin Cranston, this was a matter of death and the potential for life after death, and since Cappy Rothman had invented the postmortem sperm retrieval procedure just two years earlier, he was the only person the family could turn to.

Cappy had studied sperm enough to know that sperm motility starts declining dramatically outside of its host after forty hours. So, with no time to spare, he got into Sam, his beloved 1967 Pontiac Bonneville, and left his wife and three boys behind to enjoy their breezy Pacific Palisades house.

Sam the Pontiac (Cappy can't recall how Sam got its name) was long in the tooth and short on miles per gallon. It was also maroon with a black top. Not the best option when traveling to the desert's edge in summer, but Cappy loved that car. "We'd been together a long time" is his best explanation. Together, they soldiered into the smog, swelter, and near-apocalyptic traffic on the road from Pacific Palisades to Riverside.

Beloved as Sam may have been, the Pontiac made for quite a contrast to the fancy cars, boats, and even planes that were available to Cappy coming of age as the son of Norman "Roughhouse" Rothman, a notorious gangster during the height of mid-century Havana-Miami Beach *gangsterismo*.

From the late 1940s and into the 1960s, before he started running afoul of the law, Roughhouse rubbed shoulders with everyone from Cuban dictator Fulgencio Batista to Mob boss Santo Trafficante Jr. and even Oswald shooter Jack Ruby, if you look deep enough into conspiracy theories and internet hearsay. There was an aura around Roughhouse; some of it was as celebratory as a 1956 night in Havana, some of it as dark as *The Godfather*. Nonetheless, being "Roughhouse" Rothman's son had its advantages. Among them, it enabled Cappy to prowl South Beach in Corvettes and Cadillacs, not to mention the personal aircraft that was at Rothman's disposal.

A token of Cappy's default membership in his father's exclusive club was the 1954 bubble-top Corvette given to him after the fall of Havana by Alberto Ardura, a friend of the family and close associate of Batista's brother-in law, Roberto Fernández Miranda. The car cost about $3,000 back then but sells for more than $80,000 these days. Beauty, though, is in the eye of the beholder, and Cappy says he never liked the Corvette. "You couldn't sit up. It was small, snug, and you hit the top of your head. So, I remember giving it back to him."

Sam, on the other hand, had literally been through the fires with Cappy (more on that later) by the time they were headed to Riverside Memorial Hospital on that broiling summer day in 1982. The car had so many dings and scrapes that Cappy could no longer account for how or where most of them had been inflicted. Once, he says, he returned to the parked Pontiac after going to the market and found a note left under the wiper blade that read, "Sorry, I accidentally hit your car backing up," but Cappy couldn't tell which dent was the new one.

So, while Cappy could have, and his wife might argue should have, been driving a new, air-conditioned Cadillac, Rothman wasn't about to let his successes sway his loyalty to Sam—part of whose appeal, no doubt, was in how the car symbolized the road Cappy hadn't taken, the one his father had all but paved for him. Instead he pointed the Pontiac east on Interstate 10 toward Riverside.

The call that coaxed Cappy into the cauldron of the Inland Empire came from a powerful Boston attorney, the older sister of a young gunshot victim. Having read Cappy's papers on postmortem sperm retrieval, she wanted to know if he would go to Riverside General Hospital University Medical Center (now the Riverside University Health System—Medical Center) to retrieve the sperm from her brother, who was in a permanent vegetative state.

By this time, the California Cryobank had entered its fifth year and was starting to take off. In vitro fertilization had been a boon to the sperm-banking business, and male-factor infertility was no longer a dead end for couples hoping to conceive. Similarly, a woman who couldn't find a suitable partner was no longer sentenced to the sidelines when it came to pregnancy, birth, and motherhood. Lesbian couples looking to start families would soon increase the demand for donor sperm. Insemination techniques would also advance over the ensuing years. By 1991, it would be possible through intracytoplasmic sperm injection (ICSI) to inject a single motile sperm directly into the cytoplasm of an egg, greatly increasing the effectiveness of IVF.

Nonetheless, a postmortem sperm retrieval request was still quite novel in 1982. So novel, in fact, that Cappy didn't yet have billing protocols in place. "I was interested in it, and I couldn't say no, regardless," says Cappy. So, he cranked up the air conditioner, and he and Sam crawled along in the Los Angeles traffic.

"I was getting hot, and so was the car," recalls Cappy.

Sam started sputtering and gave out in East Los Angeles, a neighborhood that was pretty rough-and-tumble at the time. Just twenty miles into the trip, Cappy had to pull off the freeway in search of a service station. It was an inauspicious beginning to a mission that had little room for error. The clock was ticking, and every hour mattered to the viability of whatever sperm may still have been retrievable. The boy was in the intensive-care unit, brain dead but plugged into machines that kept his respiratory and cardiovascular systems operative while the family awaited Cappy's arrival.

"So I had to pull into East LA, and I think I was the only white person there. Besides that, I didn't have a tattoo," laughs Cappy, who called his wife and said, "Beth, I'm going to charge them fifty dollars, and then I'm going to come home, and we're going to go out to dinner.'"

At the service station, it became obvious that Sam's radiator had overheated. With a little coolant and water, Cappy and the Pontiac were back on the road, only now without the benefit of the air conditioner. "As I'm driving, I say, 'Well, now I'm going to charge them two hundred bucks. I mean, here I am in East LA—hazardous duty. And then the traffic got worse. By the time I got there, I was charging them fifteen hundred! At least in my mind."

Cappy may not yet have come up with a billing schedule for the procedure, but since doing the first postmortem sperm retrieval on Senator Cranston's son, and since publishing "A Method for Obtaining Viable Sperm in a Postmortem State," he had settled on some prerequisites for doing it: he wouldn't go unless he had absolute assurance that the family was in accord. He would also turn down any request that the hospital's board of directors hadn't approved ahead of time. "The CEO of Riverside General Hospital had called me before I went and said, 'Dr. Rothman, anything you need will be available; you will not have to sign anything. I can assure you this will be an expedited process," says Cappy.

The boy's mother and father greeted Cappy at the Intensive Care Unit. Cappy removed the necessary anatomy and put the organs in a cooler for the long drive back to the California Cryobank's headquarters in West Los Angeles. There, he would attempt to retrieve the sperm. The boy's mother and father followed Sam as the car gasped and sputtered back to Los Angeles.

In the much cooler confines of his office, Cappy got the anatomy ready and opened up the epididymis. He aspirated the fluid and put a sample on a slide under a microscope. Rothman invited the family to look through the microscope's lens. The deceased child's parents could see millions of motile sperm swimming all over the place, each one carrying their son's DNA. For now, anyway, death wasn't the end. Cappy looked over at the boy's mother and saw a tear trickling down her cheek.

"She gives me a kiss on the cheek and tips me a twenty," says Cappy, laughing at how the fifteen-hundred-dollar fee of his imagination had quickly turned into lunch money. But it was more than enough. "I wasn't charging anybody. I was doing it to help the family," he says.

The sperm provided some relief to the boy's family—a glimmer of light in their darkest hour. As with Senator Cranston, the parents in this case didn't end up using their son's genetic material. Importantly, though, Cappy had continued to prove the efficacy of the until-recently unprecedented procedure. It seemed inevitable that someday the ultimate reproductive frontier would be crossed, and a dead father would conceive a baby. And that Cappy Rothman would be in the middle of it.

Chapter 2
This Boy's Life

CAPPY ROTHMAN WAS BORN in the Bronx on January 12, 1938, when the country was still mired in the Great Depression. He is the eldest of three sons brought into the world by Norman and Ethel "Eddye" Rothman (née Hurowitz). In the family's early days, they lived in Apartment 2A at 1314 Hicks St., on the second floor of a walk-up near the old Boston Post Road at the northeast end of the Bronx's Williamsbridge neighborhood. Sanford "Santy" Rothman was born three years after Cappy, and Ron, three years after that. Santy died in 2012, and Ron died in the spring of 2017. A half-brother known as George or Faustino died in 1997. At eighty-four, Cappy is the last surviving sibling.

Williamsbridge took its name from eighteenth-century farmer John Williams, who kept a farm on the east bank of the Bronx River and is credited with building the first bridge over the only freshwater river in New York City. The neighborhood, now heavily populated by African Americans of Caribbean heritage, was primarily a working-class Jewish and Italian hamlet when the Rothmans lived there.

Public School 78, where Cappy attended elementary school, is still standing just a couple of blocks from the tenement where

Norman and Eddye squeezed three boys and themselves into a two-bedroom, one-bath apartment. The boys shared a room that had two beds and a mattress on the floor. Whoever got to bed last slept on the floor.

If the boys were aware that they were living through tight times in a cramped tenement, they didn't show it. Cappy had as normal a childhood as was possible for a child of first-generation Americans starting a family at the tail end of the Great Depression. Rothman describes himself as an energetic and mischievous boy who spent his time in the neighborhood playing stickball and handball, flipping cards, and shooting marbles. If the weather wasn't suitable, or he couldn't muster a game, Cappy would hit the corner candy shop on the way to the movies, where he'd catch up on serials such as *Captain America*, *Brenda Starr*, *The Sea Hound*, and the like. Sometimes he'd take in a double feature.

Cappy took guitar lessons as a boy; at least until that winter's day he thought it would be a good idea to use his guitar case to slide down a snow-covered Boston Post Road. "I broke it, and my parents were very annoyed," he says. "And that was the end of my musical career."

He also kept eleven garden snakes in a fish tank and remembers well the time all but two escaped while he was cleaning the tank. "I heard this tremendous scream from the neighbors downstairs…they went down the pipes," Cappy laughs. "At one time, I liked snakes. I don't know why. I don't like them now."

During the war years, Cappy recalls, "We had to take our bubblegum and put it in the refrigerator and put sugar on it to keep it going. You'd take the tinfoil from the gum and make a ball and turn it in to the government agency, and they'd take the tin."

He also developed a fondness for White Castle, which brought to the hamburger business what Ford brought to the automobile industry: mass assembly. White Castle sliders cost just five cents in the forties, and if he had some change, Cappy says, "I could eat three to seven."

Traveling back decades in time and across the continent from his sunny Pacific Palisades perch, Cappy remembers watching the first televised heavyweight boxing match at his uncle's house down the street. The fight pitted Joe Louis against Billy Conn in the June 19, 1946, rematch of their classic 1941 bout, wherein Conn, a light-heavyweight champ, had challenged the Brown Bomber during the great heavyweight's prime. Most scorekeepers had Conn comfortably ahead in the thirteenth round when he foolishly tired himself by "being too Irish" and going for a knockout. Instead, Louis knocked him out.

The two boxers then went into the service. While Conn went off to war and didn't return until 1946, Louis was used for recruitment, morale, and fund-raising purposes. After the war, the public clamored for a rematch, even though the layoff had sapped their skills. This time, Louis knocked Conn out in the eighth round. About 141,000 people, including Cappy Rothman, saw the fight on NBC. It was the largest fight audience to date.

Roughhousing seemed to run in the family. Cappy recalls an incident when he and his brother Santy were jumping from the bureau onto the mattresses that were on the floor while the bed frames were getting fixed. A large fish tank that was home to about thirty pet fish occupied most of the space on top of the bureau. During one of his leaps, Cappy kicked the tank, smashing it and sending fish flopping all over the room.

"I remember my mom and dad picking up the mattress and trying to catch the fish between the coils," Cappy says, laughing at the image of his father with a little fishnet trying to save the fish while his mom tended to his lacerated foot. "I was held over the toilet while my mom poured hydrogen peroxide on my cut." The wound ended up requiring stitches, but Cappy wasn't the only casualty.

"The neighbors complained when the water from the tank started leaking through the ceiling. But they complained more when the snakes went down the pipes," says Cappy.

Though the Rothmans were far from well off, Cappy insists he never felt anything like deprivation during his early days in the Bronx. "We were middle class," he says.

Or at least middle-class enough for the occasional family trip to the Catskills—one of which was interrupted when Cappy got the mumps. "They kind of snuck me out of the hotel in the middle of the night," he remembers with a chuckle. "They didn't want anyone to know someone was there with an infectious disease."

In school, Cappy had yet to develop the academic acumen he displayed later in life. Some of that may have had to do with being left-handed. Back then, it was viewed as an affliction, something to be corrected. Cappy was forced to do everything right-handed, including write. "It was hard to be a lefty in 1942 at PS 78," Cappy says. "Being a lefty wasn't really acceptable. They tried to make you a righty."

On the bright side, Rothman says the experience may have helped him develop some of the ambidexterity that would give him an advantage later in life when it came to performing delicate microsurgeries, including vasectomies and vasectomy reversals.

Another hallmark of Cappy's childhood was his battles with an unusual condition known as cold urticaria, which would cause him to break out in hives and develop itchy, swelling skin during the winter. He was literally allergic to the cold, practically the only thing that was in abundant supply during those long Bronx winters. That may explain why he was relatively unruffled when, at age ten, he was told the family would be moving to Miami Beach. A move that would coincide with his father's transformation from Norman Rothman to Norman "Roughhouse" Rothman.

◇

CAPPY'S FATHER, NORMAN ROTHMAN, was drafted into the Army in March 1945, near the end of World War II. He was honorably discharged the following December 19, just two and half months after Japan surrendered. By now, Norman Rothman was thirty-one years old and had three boys aged seven, four, and one. His military service is a bit puzzling, considering the age at which he was drafted and the brevity of his service stint, though conscription wasn't officially suspended until 1946. His Army service, though, may be part of a bigger puzzle, along with old neighborhood ties and his ensuing years as a union man.

What is clear is that by 1947, Rothman had found his way into a stake in the Cocktail Lounge at the Albion Hotel on Lincoln Road and James Avenue in South Beach, Miami Beach. The Albion, a masterpiece of art deco designed by the famed architect Ygor Polivirsky, boasted the best amenities of its time, including a private pool. It was the epitome of South Beach's midcentury gangster chic, the era that the short-lived cable series *Magic City* tried to emulate.

While *Magic City* was fiction, the Albion Lounge was indeed a gangster hangout. Whether Norman Rothman knew it when he got involved with the enterprise is not entirely clear, but Rothman's FBI files, obtained through a Freedom of Information Act request, indicate that by this time he was already friendly with Gabriel "Kelly" Mannarino and his brother Sam, members of the Pittsburgh crime family headed by John Sebastian LaRocca.

The Mannarinos were former bootleggers, and Gabriel, in particular, was known for his Midas touch. Pittsburgh boss LaRocca took a shine to the boys and helped them expand their enterprises. Soon, they were running all the rackets in New Kensington, a once-bustling industrial city and birthplace of the giant aluminum company Alcoa. Sam would run afoul of both the law and his crime family, but his brother would continue to ascend within LaRocca's organization and was soon a capo.

Perhaps Rothman got mixed up with the Mannarinos during his days as a construction industry labor relations representative in New York in the early 1940s. Regardless, Cappy remembers there were always plenty of Catoris Candies chocolate turtles around the house, which were made in New Kensington and were favored by Gabriel Mannarino, who had a notorious sweet tooth and way with the ladies, despite his diminutive stature (5'5") and excessive weight (190). Gabriel also had growing interests in Florida and Havana and had bought stakes in legal Cuban casinos in the late forties and early fifties, including the San Souci. He was known to have deployed "a versatile Florida-based hood named Norman Rothman as a shill and a frontman," as one Mafia-focused website put it.

Cappy suspects that his father started his gangster career as the Albion Lounge's bookie. "Dad started in Cuba in the late forties. I think he was probably a bookie—I don't know for sure—and at the Albion, where he made some contacts, met some people, and then went to Cuba," says Cappy. "I went to Cuba for the first time when I was twelve or thirteen. That would have been 1950 or 1951."

Norman's connections with the Mannarinos would eventually pave the way for him to take over as manager of the Sans Souci nightclub and casino in Cuba when the Mannarinos went into business there with South Florida Mob boss Santo Trafficante Jr. By then, Norman Rothman was known as Norman "Roughhouse" Rothman and had a seat at the tables of prominent members of La Cosa Nostra. The Mannarino brothers, along with other gangster luminaries, would attend Cappy's wedding to his wife, Beth, some twenty years after Norman Rothman and Eddye moved to Miami Beach in 1948, back when it was all just getting started.

⌒

WHEN THE FAMILY MOVED, Cappy was ten—a tough age for a kid making a big change. By first and second grade, kids generally start making connections to people and places, with friends being the most significant. Of course, that can be balanced by a keen sense of adventure, and that seems to have been the case with Cappy. "I was disappointed to leave my friends and the life I had, not knowing where I was going, but it was exciting to go to a new place with the weather and the water," he says. "I think I was more excited than disappointed."

He remembers flying to Miami, with his pet turtles in tow, to the new experience of Southern segregation. "The bathrooms were colored and white, and 'the coloreds' sat in the back of the bus and had to be off Miami Beach by twelve o'clock," recalls Cappy.

If South Florida was unsettling in some ways that a ten-year-old from the Bronx would notice but might find hard to articulate, in other ways it offered everything a boy could want: surf, sand, and civilization that ended abruptly at a canal or the edge of the swamp or the oceanfront. Fishing, hunting, boating, swimming, and adventuring beckoned amid the half-built promise of a semitropical paradise. There is perhaps nothing more adaptable than a ten-year-old boy, and after the initial culture shock wore off, Cappy resumed his rambunctious *Boys' Life* youth—albeit with fewer outbreaks of cold urticaria.

"We moved from New York down to Miami Beach, and I don't remember the address, but it was two blocks off Collins Avenue [the main drag] to Byron and Ninety-First Street, because we could walk to the beach very easily. There were two little bungalows. We had one of them, and my father's friend Ben Wolf and his wife, Molly, had the other one. They had children close to our age. There was a big palmetto field next to our house. It was totally underdeveloped, and it was fun," recalls Cappy. "I had a pet chicken I named Chicken that would follow me around...I remember collecting bottles from the beach to buy a bow and arrows. I think you got one or two cents a bottle."

Interesting characters thrived in mid-century Florida, and there was always some adventure ready. Cappy recalls the Perez brothers, who imported exotic animals from Central and South America to sell to zoos and to people who wanted showy pets. Cappy went to work for the Perez brothers in his late teens and would often pick up the animals from the airport holding cages and then deliver them.

Although he didn't know it at the time, Cappy was developing what would become his lifelong interest in healing. He set up a makeshift infirmary in his garage that served as part veterinarian office and part wildlife refuge. "Any animal that was sick, I was able to bring home and try to nurse it back to health," says Cappy, "I had the opportunity to really learn about the animals of South America."

Cappy says he handled about fifteen different species of monkeys and at various times was the caretaker of capuchin monkeys (the organ-grinder monkeys), spider monkeys, marmosets, and squirrel monkeys, as well as a variety of other mammals, birds, and fish.

"When I started the University of Miami, I had my own monkey, Lanky. He looked like Jerry Lewis. He was a spider monkey, and he would wrap his tail around my wrist. He accompanied me in my brand-new Ford convertible when I went to school. I trained Lanky to put the money in the net when we went through the Venetian Causeway toll bridge. While I was in class, he stayed in the car, attracting a significant amount of attention. Unfortunately, the police came and made us get rid of Lanky after he caused a couple of accidents by hanging from the telephone wires at intersections and distracting the drivers who saw him," says Cappy, laughing. "I had an ocelot at one point and coatimundis, kinkajous, and numerous other animals from Central and South America."

Now, Cappy looks back on those times with a certain nostalgia. "I wish my kids could have been brought up in the same era I was brought up," he says. "It was warmer, friendlier, more fun, and I think easier, even though we didn't have air conditioning and there were mosquitos."

During his early teen years, Cappy says, he sometimes worked as a cabana boy, "smoothing out the beaches." But things were not always smooth at school. Cappy started getting in trouble soon after the family moved to Miami Beach. "I don't remember being in trouble with the police," he says, "but I do remember not being amenable to authority, any type of authority. School was not a happy place for me."

There were also the growing absences of his father to contend with. Norman Rothman's "work" had him splitting time between Miami and Havana. It's easy to connect Cappy's budding rebelliousness with resentments he may have harbored, however inarticulately, to being uprooted and to his father's growing absences. But when presented with this possibility, Rothman pauses as if pondering it for the first time. "I would say yes," he eventually replies, though unconvinced. "I didn't know at the time he [Roughhouse] was leading a double life," he adds.

Nor did he know the extent of it.

Nonetheless, Cappy's issues with authority figures extended even to his intimidating father. After one particular disagreement, he informed his family he was running away to California to become a rancher, which makes some sense given his love of animals. Young Cappy grew especially fond of horses and developed into a competitive rider. But as far as his threat went, his father told Cappy that he was fine with it and that he would provide a one-way ticket. So, Cappy ran away to a motel down the street, where he stayed for a few weeks while his mother brought him meals and did his laundry.

Maybe because he saw too much of himself in his eldest son, or maybe because he didn't want him to see too much of his own other life, Norman Rothman enrolled Cappy in military school when Cappy turned twelve. Cappy attended Riverside Military Academy, where he split time between the campuses at Gainesville, Georgia, and Hollywood, Florida, for a year before transferring to Valley Forge Military Academy in Wayne, Pennsylvania, from which he graduated. "It was either that [military school] or reform school," Cappy says.

Between the ages of twelve and seventeen, Cappy would spend nine months of the year away in military school. If that was meant to set Cappy straight, it didn't exactly work. Not at first, anyway. Even in the strict confines of the military academies, Cappy says he was rebellious. It was a bearing that earned him repeated trips to "the bullring" at Riverside, where misbehaving cadets were run through extra drills and exercises. Cappy insists he wasn't so much a bad kid as a rambunctious one; someone we'd probably diagnose with attention-deficit/ hyperactivity disorder today.

He didn't fare much better with authority when he moved on to Valley Forge. Cappy says his approach to military school, like his approach to authority in general, was less compliant than his friends'. "When they [authority figures] weren't looking, I was a little less of an automaton," he says.

Of Fred Fields, his old roommate from Valley Forge, Cappy says, "They probably put us together because we were both Jewish. When we first met, we didn't get along because he was Mr. Goody Two Shoes, and I was there in lieu of reform school."

Despite his many trips to the bullring, Cappy managed to get basic junior ROTC training at military school along with a rigorous academic schedule that would prepare him for when he was finally able to focus his attention. Still, he says, "I started my last year of military school as a [cadet] lieutenant but finished as a sergeant, so I must have done something wrong."

One thing he did right was to learn how to ride horses. At Valley Forge, Cappy became a member of the horsemanship specialty program known as D Troop. Members learned cavalry skills, show jumping, parading, fox hunting, and competitive equitation. "I loved riding and spending my time in the stables. I was one of the best riders," says Cappy. "That, I was exceptional at."

He fondly remembers Rubberneck, the thoroughbred who could turn his head almost 180 degrees when you pulled on the reins. "He would run into walls," says Cappy. And Big Ben, the Clydesdale draught horse who was bought by a Pabst Blue Ribbon heiress and renamed Peoria Pabst, even though the heiress and horse lived in Connecticut. "He was a big monster of a horse," Cappy recalls.

He rode the horse on the jumping circuit one summer in the employ of the Pabst heiress after her rider broke his arm taking a jump with Big Ben. Cappy was a good enough rider to earn a spot in the Harriers' Club, the elite riders of D Troop. D Troop competed in the Intercollegiate Horse Show Association as well as in local horse shows and in events the Valley Forge Military hosted. Cappy competed in the open-jumping circuit and even in a bronco-riding event at a rodeo.

Perhaps the most surprising thing about his military academy experience is that Rothman became a competitive polo player. This is a rare feat for left-handers since polo ponies are almost exclusively trained for righties. Cappy got in the saddle when Sam Weatherall, a fellow lefty, broke his arm. Weatherall's horses had been trained to approach the ball from a southpaw perspective.

"I don't remember school or classes, but I remember a lot about the horses," Cappy says. "I do remember getting on a horse and becoming one with a horse. Sitting on a horse, bareback, Western saddle, Eastern saddle, McClellan saddle [used by the cavalry], and knowing where we were going."

Norman "Roughhouse" Rothman took great pride in seeing his eldest boy smartly turned out in uniform and wasn't shy about showing off his tall, good-looking son around Cuba during the summers when Cappy would join his father there. "I remember actually having a picture, maybe for New Year's Eve, when I was in my Riverside Uniform, and I remember we were staying at Hotel Nacional," says Cappy. The picture is from 1955. "Cuba was totally different then," he says.

It certainly was.

Chapter 3

Son of a Roughhouse

WHEN CAPPY VISITED CUBA as a boy, the island was still mostly an incubator for American imperial interests, whether sugar barons or mafiosi. It had been much that way since the 1898 Spanish-American War all but codified US dominion over Cuba. The Mafia, for its part, had been coveting the island as a money-laundering machine and putting its tentacles into every layer of society even before Prohibition. Its progress toward a mid-fifties Havana heyday, though, had come in fits and starts.

The prestigious Hotel Nacional de Cuba, where Cappy stayed with his father, figured prominently in the Mafia's vision for Cuba. The hotel became the launching pad for the modern gangster era, which reached its peak under Cuban dictator Fulgencio Batista, when nearly two dozen of America's most important Mob bosses gathered there on December 22, 1946.

The pretext for the gathering was Frank Sinatra's Havana debut, though Sinatra wasn't the main attraction. The assembled gangsters had more important things on their minds. The summit had been called by Meyer Lansky, who, along with Charles "Lucky" Luciano, was most responsible for revamping the old-school La Cosa Nostra ("our thing") into the more modern, businesslike National Crime Syndicate—a term coined by the Senate subcommittee headed by Tennessee Senator Estes Kefauver, who in the early fifties chaired a senate committee investigating the Mob.

Lansky and Luciano were leaders of a new generation of Mafia known as the Young Turks. Unlike their predecessors, who mostly came from Sicily and who wanted to limit business to an inner circle with ties to the old country, the Young Turks were mostly American born, or at least Americanized. They viewed their operations through the more transactional lens of global business. If it made bottom line sense, they were open to collaborating with Jews, Irish...whoever was good for business. Aside from a shared interest in professionalizing their criminal activities, Lansky and Luciano also coveted the opportunities presented by Havana, where gambling on horses, on jai alai, and in a limited number of casinos, had been permitted since 1915.

At the top of the to-do list for the Young Turks attending the 1946 Hotel Nacional conference was Lanksy's long-standing desire to turn Cuba, and Havana, in particular, into something like a Syndicate holding company. He envisioned a country all but run by the Mob, with its fingers on all the levers of society from business to infrastructure building to banking and, of course, gambling and tourism. Cuba was to be both a massive source of revenue and a money-laundering machine. That, essentially, was the pitch Lansky made at Hotel Nacional that week.[1]

Norman Rothman was one of the more enigmatic figures of this colorful era. Not only was he a physically big man, he had a very large presence. When he was summoned and questioned by the senators and congressmen about the Cuban Missile Crisis, they treated him with respect and appreciated his knowledge about Castro, the revolution, the people involved, and Cuba. Cappy was present at the senate hearings, the only time he got to observe his father as a key government witness, and one of the many times, he felt impressed by him.

Norman Rothman seemed always to be in the thick of things but hardly ever the center of attention. Rothman may not have been at the Hotel Nacional to hear the Cuba pitch, but he would soon start playing a more visible supporting role to gangster dons such as Lansky and Santo Trafficante Jr. At one point, Rothman managed all of the slot machines in Cuba outside of Havana proper, and it's hard to imagine he didn't get a decent slice of that pie.

Rothman had a reputation as someone who could get things done, whether it was running the Havana slots or the Sans Souci nightclub. The FBI compiled a thick file on him and almost certainly had him under surveillance at various times during his life. The FBI lists among his close friends such notorious gangsters as Trafficante Jr., Sam and Gabriel Mannarino, and Pasquale "Paddy" Erra, a soldier in the Genovese crime family whose connections to Rothman may go back to New York.

When exactly Cappy's father became "Roughhouse" Rothman is unclear, but it's not hard to imagine how a first-generation Jewish boy growing up in the Bronx without much of an education and with few resources to call upon needed to be tough to get by. Rothman, apparently, didn't waste any time letting the mean streets of the South Bronx know he was not to be trifled with. He carried that trait with him his entire life. "My mom said that more than half the times she went out with my dad, he would get into a fight, and she would wind up coming home by herself," says Cappy. "Ergo his name, 'Roughhouse.'"

In the 1950s and 1960s, when "Roughhouse" earned most of his notoriety, the Mafia was still minted in the public's imagination by Hollywood and Broadway versions of Damon Runyon characters played by the likes of James Cagney, George Raft, and Humphrey Bogart. *Guys and Dolls* premiered on Broadway in 1950, and the film version starring Marlon Brando and Frank Sinatra came out in 1955. As the sixties turned to the seventies and the Mafia got more into drug trafficking, a harsher assessment took hold in books and films, such as

The Godfather, *The French Connection*, *Mean Streets*, and later, *Goodfellas*. Norman Rothman's underworld career, dating back at least to when he took a stake in the Albion Lounge in 1947, spanned that transition.

During his life, Roughhouse would rack up felony convictions for attempting to run guns stolen from a National Guard Armory in Ohio into Cuba and for conspiring to transport and fence millions of dollars in securities stolen from a Canadian bank. Those were the major beefs noted in his FBI jacket, but there were other arrests and indictments. The FBI identifies him as a loan shark, an extortionist, a shot-caller and fence for a jewelry-theft ring, and someone who always carried a sidearm, among other things.

Association, innuendo, and sometimes actions also implicated Rothman in schemes to get money and weapons to Batista loyalists after Castro seized power. If you crawl deep enough into Mafia-aficionado websites, you'll find Rothman linked to the Bay of Pigs invasion, Jack Ruby, the Kennedy assassination, and many of the Mob's signature events from its heyday.

~

So, who exactly is Cappy's father? FBI notes and records, indictments, and gossipy gangster-focused websites paint a murky picture of someone who was a venerable presence in the fifties and sixties mob scene and an associate of some of the highest profile gangsters of his day, yet who always remained somewhat in the background. He appears to be a high-level, second-tier guy; someone who had a seat at the table but was never really at the head of it.

Norman Rothman was born on December 26, 1914, to Leon Rothman and Betty Rothman (formerly Tannenbaum). Leon's and Betty's parents had emigrated from Romania during the tail end of a huge Jewish exodus from Eastern Europe as the shadow of war and anti-Semitic violence swept the continent. Like plenty of immigrants before and after them, the Rothmans didn't arrive in the New World wealthy. Norman, the eldest son, went to work at an early age.

As a teen, Norman Rothman falsified his birth date to secure a job at F. W. Woolworth Company on Westchester Avenue in the Bronx. By eighteen, he was helping to dig the foundation for Radio City Music Hall at Rockefeller Center as a rock-driller's assistant. He continued to find employment in construction during the Depression, when public works projects were some of the few reliable jobs available.

Rothman eventually took a job with the Rusoff Construction Company, which specialized in subway construction and infrastructure. He labored on sewer lines in Manhattan and worked on building the New York City Subway's Sixth Avenue Line. Severe headaches and a case of the bends contracted while working underground, however, moved Rothman aboveground and into more supervisory roles.

It was around then, according to notes for an intended autobiography Rothman began compiling while in prison, that the young man became "interested in the union cause" and helped organize laborers working on the Sixth Avenue Line. He must have been effective, because after the subway opened in 1936, Rusoff transferred Rothman to upstate New York, where he took the role of head timekeeper for field operations—a job that called for him to be the company's union liaison.

With the 1939 World's Fair coming to Flushing Meadows Corona Park, Rothman was tapped to be the president and general business agent for the World's Fair Union. When the World's Fair closed in 1940, he wrote that he went to work as an engineer at the Military Ocean Terminal in Bayonne, New Jersey, a naval dry dock just getting under construction. Rothman contracted bronchial pneumonia, though, and had to leave the job.

Norman Rothman resumed work as a labor-relations man for a construction company before doing a short stint in the

Army between March and December 1945. Following his honorable discharge, Rothman returned to the Bronx with his wife, Ethel "Eddye" Rothman, and their three sons. Ethel was the daughter of Morris and Rebecca Hurowitz, who had escaped from Russia and had also landed in the Bronx.

How Norman Rothman occupied himself in the first years after his brief Army service is unclear, but he writes that it was at Miami Beach's Albion Lounge that he "became friendly" with several Cubans. The friendliness led to Rothman visiting Cuba in 1948. "This turned out to be a business trip," wrote Rothman, "as I bought into the Sans Souci Nightclub, Restaurant, and Casino, where gambling had just become legalized."

The major players in the Sans Souci at the time were Gabriel "Kelly" Mannarino and his brother Sam, who took a liking to Rothman, as did Santo Trafficante Jr. The FBI believes the Mannarino brothers were Rothman's financial backers as he looked to opportunities in Cuba's legal, but corrupt, gambling business. Trafficante Jr. would soon buy the majority interest in the Sans Souci in 1953. He was a key figure in the new wave of American and Cuban *gangsterismo* that saw both Cuban and American mobsters form partnerships with dictator Fulgencio Batista after the 1952 coup that put Batista back in power. According to T. J. English's definitive account of the era, *Havana Nocturne*, this at long last consummated a courtship between the American mob and Cuba that Meyer Lansky had been nurturing since 1933.

Meyer Lansky, one of the most prominent mid-century mob figures first began making overtures to Batista at the end of Prohibition and the nadir of the Great Depression. Batista was then something of a minor, if rising star, in Cuban politics. When Batista took power during the 1933 "Revolt of the Sergeants," the Mob's designs on Cuba seemed primed to come true. Cuba had sun, surf, beautiful people, lots of resources, and a scarcity of what the American Mafia did have—cash. All the Mafia needed was a willing accomplice, and they found their man in Batista.

A case can be made that Batista, a strange mix of autocrat and populist, took power with some good intentions—among them modernizing and stabilizing a country that had a history of political turmoil and factional violence in the power vacuum left after Cuba finally gained independence from Spain in 1898. Batista attempted to consolidate and legitimize his power after the "Revolt of the Sergeants" by holding open elections in 1940. He won the presidency more or less fairly on a platform to enact the progressive constitution he had adopted during his military regime.

Batista's presidency, though, didn't survive the next election in 1944, when he lost to Ramón Grau's Auténtico-Republica party. Batista spent the next eight years in semi-exile, hopping between the Waldorf Astoria in New York and a house he kept in Daytona Beach. During this period, he divorced his first wife and married Marta Fernandez, who gave birth to two of their four kids in the US. It's a good bet that Batista's connections to Santo Trafficante Jr. and other influential South Florida mobsters grew even closer during this time.

While living in Daytona, Batista ran for a seat in the Cuban Senate in 1948 and won. He decided to run for president again in 1951, but when polls showed him losing disastrously to then president Carlos Prío Socorrás, Batista engineered a second military coup on March 10, 1952. The US wasted no time officially recognizing the government of its old friend and biggest regional trading partner.

This time around, Batista swapped his progressive posturing for a full-on tin-pot dictatorship. He focused on currying favor with wealthy landowners and businessmen, selling off resources to US-based companies, and getting in bed with the American Mafia, which took over the hotel, casino, and gaming operations as well as the narcotics and prostitution trades.

The time was finally ripe for the Mafia's dream of turning Havana into a Las Vegas or Monte Carlo in the Caribbean. Under Batista's new regime, anyone who invested either

$200,000 in a nightclub or $1 million in a hotel got a gaming license without any hassle. What's more, Cuba would match foreign investments above $1 million with state subsidies. Much of this foreign investment came from the Mob. Lansky and colleagues even opened up banks in Havana to keep the capital circulating.

The gaming, tourism, and illicit trade money flowed freely to the ruling class and its Mafia partners, but Havana's organized-crime makeover failed to benefit the poor, rural agricultural areas. And that was where a young, upper-class revolutionary named Fidel Castro started fomenting revolution almost as soon as Batista took back control of Cuba in 1952.

∽

Meanwhile, Santo Trafficante Jr., the Tampa, Florida, Mob boss who, along with his legendary father, Santo Sr., had long run the numbers rackets in the thriving Cuban section of Tampa, knew the culture of Cuba well. With Batista back in power, he bought his majority stake in the Sans Souci from the Mannarino brothers and also had stakes in the Comodoro and Capri Hotels.

In a bit of life imitating art, actor George Raft, who played tough-guy mobsters in forties films such as the original *Scarface*, owned a piece of the Capri, where Trafficante Jr. installed him as an official greeter. Wannabe gangsters had been copping Raft's onscreen style for years, and now here he was, renting his faux-gangster persona out to the real ones.

Sometimes, though, things got too real. One of Cappy's early teen memories of visiting Cuba involves being in an elevator with Raft at Meyer Lansky's famous Havana Riviera. "We hear machine guns, and we both hit the floor," says Cappy, who can't remember the source or cause of the gunfire, though gunfire wasn't an uncommon sound in Havana then.

Cappy's father had been running the Sans Souci for the Mannarinos by the time Trafficante got hold of it. The Sans Souci ("carefree") dated back to the World War I era and was located seven miles outside of Havana in a lush, wooded area. It was known for its *bolita* operation (a lottery-type numbers racket) and its entertainment.

In order to encourage tourists to travel outside Havana proper, the Sans Souci needed to provide a little extra incentive. To do that, it developed a reputation for putting on the best floorshows in Cuba. Santo Trafficante Jr. refurbished the casino and, at Meyer Lansky's urging, cleaned up the "razzle-dazzle" scams (rigged games) prevalent at casinos in the forties and early fifties. The thinking was simple: cleaner gambling and world-class entertainment would turn Cuba into a destination for cosmopolitan tourists who wanted to rumba in the tropics, not the desert. Casino revenues during the Batista era would bear out this judgment.

An odd anecdote involving "Roughhouse" Rothman and Dana C. Smith, a fund-raiser turned adviser to Vice President Richard Nixon, may have added urgency to Lansky's order to clean things up. The Nixon operative apparently got caught up in a bit of razzle-dazzle called *cubolo*, an eight-dice casino game, while visiting Havana in April 1952 and gambling at the San Souci. Pit bosses urged Smith to double down on each loss, and he ended up owing the house $4,200 (about $26,000 today). Smith dutifully wrote a check. Later, perhaps after sobering up, he realized he'd been taken to the cleaners and canceled the check.

In a display of bravado or foolishness, "Roughhouse" Rothman sued Smith in a Los Angeles court to retrieve the money. Nixon brought the weight of the State Department to bear on the matter, and needless to say, Rothman lost the case. The attention paid to the case by the press, though, did spark a firestorm of complaints from tourists saying they'd been similarly duped in Havana. The scandal coincided with a downturn in tourism. Havana officially noted there might be some merit to the complaints and casino operators got the message to clean up the razzle-dazzle.

Despite losing the Smith case, "Roughhouse" Rothman still had a way of getting things done. When the Mob-run Havana casinos got the green light to put in slot machines, Rothman arranged to have thousands procured through his gangster associations around the US—most notably the Mannarino brothers. Rothman's FBI documents reference Miami agents seizing a raft of illegal slot machines sent to Rothman's Surfside Miami home by the Mannarinos.

Despite such setbacks, Rothman was able to commandeer enough slots to get the party rolling in Havana, and he was rewarded for his efforts. After Trafficante Jr. took over the Sans Souci, he kept Rothman onboard to run the casino floor and oversee the entertainment. According to his FBI files, Rothman also controlled all the slots outside of Havana.

Under Rothman, the San Souci put on the best Cuban cabaret and attracted international stars such as Dorothy Dandridge, Marlene Dietrich, Edith Piaf, Liberace, and more. The revues were extravagant and would feature dozens of dancers. The two best known were "Bamba Iroko Bamba" and "Sun Sun Babae," one of the biggest shows ever staged in Cuba. Cappy recalls seeing his father having dinner with Burt Lancaster at the San Souci. He also recalls seeing Ernest Hemingway, who was living in Cuba at the time, while writing *The Old Man and the Sea*. Both Hemingway and Douglas Fairbanks Jr., one of Cappy's movie idols, were heavy drinkers and gamblers.

Roderico Neyra, a flamboyant and brilliant choreographer, built these shows around Afro-Cuban bada drums, adding kitschy elements of Santeria and voodoo to the spicy mix. In "Sun Sun Babae," a plant in the audience (often a blonde dancer from New Jersey named Skippy) would appear to get swept into an erotic fervor by the drumbeats and the dancing until she ended up in a trance onstage, ready to be carried off into a carnal night.

Skippy wasn't the only one getting swept away by Cuban delights. Norman Rothman spent a lot of time at the Sans Souci's main rival for top hot spot, the Tropicana. The rivalry was mitigated somewhat by Trafficante Jr. also having a stake in the Tropicana. Trafficante Jr. reportedly inserted longtime Jack Ruby associate Lewis McWillie as the manager at one point, but Cuban gambler/gangster Martin Fox was the Tropicana's nominal owner.

Rothman, no doubt, had plenty of business reasons to check in at the Tropicana—he had supplied it with its slot machines, for instance—but he had another compelling interest, too. Her name was Olga Chaviano, the so-called "Queen of the Mambo," a dark-haired beauty who had danced with "Sun Sun Babae" at the Sans Souci in the past before migrating to the Tropicana with Neyra in the early fifties.

Chaviano had started dancing professionally when she was fifteen and became a star of stage and screen. Though married to her dance partner, "Chaviano was courted by the richest and most influential men of the time," according to her IMDB bio. "Roughhouse" Rothman was neither the richest nor the most influential, but he must have had something going for him because before long Chaviano was Rothman's girl. For many years, Rothman would lead a second life, fathering a son, Faustino "George" Rothman, and keeping a house in the Cuban countryside with the Queen of the Mambo.

When asked, Cappy Rothman is almost stubbornly nonjudgmental about his father's dual career and family lives. To him, "Roughhouse" was a charismatic figure and a sometime source of reflected glamour and privilege. At the very least, he exposed Cappy to a less ordinary life, one in which he met the likes of Batista's brother-in-law, General Roberto Fernández Miranda ("a good-looking, big man"), during his summer trips to Cuba. Cappy remembers how the Cubans all carried .45 pistols, many customized with pearl- and gold-plated handles, and how they would place them on special shelves built into the dining tables around which they usually met. Havana mobster Alberto Adura was just "part of the family."

As a kid, Cappy says, he was vaguely aware that his father was what they called a gangster, something he would become increasingly aware of as he grew older, but when he was still in school, Cappy says, "I was in military school from the ages of twelve to seventeen, so I was away a lot. I was only home in the summer, and then I would go to Cuba. I knew he had another family in Cuba that I never told my mother about…though my mother knew something."

In Havana, at least, it would have been hard to predict the coming scarcities of Castro's Cuba from inside the intoxicating excesses of the Batista era. Cappy would visit Norman Rothman's house near Camagüey, just outside of Havana, during the summers. It's easy to imagine what it must have looked like to a teenage Cappy Rothman—the whirlwind of exotic showgirls, known as *las diosas de carne* (flesh goddesses), dressed in sequins, feathers, and not much more; the Cuban rhythms during the late-night revues; and the roster of international stars such as Nat King Cole, Carmen Miranda, Edith Piaf, Dorothy Dandridge, Tony Martin, and his beautiful wife, Cyd Charisse, whose legs were insured for $5 million in the 1950s. Cappy admits to having a crush on Charisse at the time. From his perspective, "the insurance policy was undervalued."

Being the oldest and favored son of Norman Rothman had its privileges. As a young man, Cappy Rothman befriended Batista's son, Jorge, and would occasionally go with his father to meet the boss, Santo Trafficante Jr., in Miami. When he was a little older, in the days before the Batista regime came crashing down in '59 when Cappy was twenty-one, his visits to Cuba included raucous nights of partying with the sons of the political, cultural, and *gangsterismo* elite. He earned the nickname "Flaca" for his preference for slender women, while his Cuban friends preferred *culas grandes* (big butts).

"I was friendly with the sons of the affluent. These were just hell-raising guys. There would be a caravan of cars because they had their bodyguards with them," says Cappy. "I know there were a lot of women, there were a lot of shows, there was a lot of dancing and a lot of drinking. I never got into the drinking, but I got into the women."

Rothman, whether looking back with rose-tinted nostalgia or not, remembers his father being beloved in Cuba. "Whenever I was in one of the clubs in Havana and there would be the music and the entertainment, and then there'd suddenly be a little segment of 'Sun Sun Babae,' I'd know my father had entered the club. It wasn't the owners of the club; it was the musicians. He was so well-loved in Havana that just walking down the street, the guys who would do your shoes would say, 'Hi, Mr. Normie!' And if he got the little Cuban coffee, they all knew him. They all loved him. He was Mr. Normie to everybody—from his drivers, to the people who worked for him, to the people he worked for."

Cappy says he met his half-brother, Faustino, in Havana in 1955, when Faustino, or George as he was called, was still a toddler. Cappy was seventeen and had just graduated from Valley Forge Military Academy and was spending the summer in Cuba with his father. One day Roughhouse took Cappy to an apartment he kept in town. "My father looked at me and said, 'I want you to meet your brother George…and don't tell your mother.'"

For a stark illustration of the separate but connected lives Cappy and Faustino led, consider the parallel graduation parties the two half-brothers held one week apart in 1969 at the famed Eden Roc Miami Beach Hotel. There, Faustino celebrated making it through high school while Cappy marked his graduation from medical school. "George had the Cuban family, plus friends, and I had the American family, plus friends. Same venue, different people," deadpans Cappy.

A go-to-venue for the Rothmans, a few years later, the Eden Roc would also host Norman Rothman's release-from-prison party after he completed a five-year bid for multiple federal counts of possession, transportation, and conspiracy relating to stolen securities.

Cappy didn't see Faustino again until Faustino came out to California and visited Cappy and Beth at their first home in Pacific Palisades many years later. Beth was told he was a family friend. Faustino wound up spending the night and sleeping in the boys' room. In the morning, Michael asked why Daddy was sleeping in their room. It didn't take long for Beth to ask who this Faustino really was! The half-brothers saw each other intermittently but didn't forge a tight bond during Faustino's short life. Neither of Cappy's brothers, Sanford "Santy" nor Ronnie, managed to develop a relationship with Faustino, and the subject of Roughhouse Rothman's double life and whatever pain or discomfort it caused seems to have been dulled by time or buried in denial. It was not a favored topic among Cappy's brothers when they were living. The sole surviving sibling, Cappy says: "My father had a family in Cuba and a family here, and probably when he was flying, thirty-five minutes into the flight, he changed the pictures in his wallet."

Olga Chaviano and Faustino eventually fled Castro's Cuba in 1966, and Olga managed to continue dancing in Miami, New York, Los Angeles, and Las Vegas, joined onstage frequently by her son, who became a dancer in his own right. Olga Chaviano had the misfortune of outliving her son, who died of AIDS in 1997, at the age of forty-one. Olga Chaviano died five years later of pneumonia in 2003 while being treated for a brain tumor.

Chapter 4

Pre-Med

CAPPY ROTHMAN GRADUATED FROM Valley Forge Military Academy in 1955 and enrolled at the University of Miami, where he joined the Reserve Officer Training Corps (ROTC). The ROTC trains future military officers and asks members to commit to active duty in the service after college in exchange for a military commission and avoidance of being drafted.

Rothman would take his time with higher education, dabbling in everything from architecture to business. What was the rush, after all? He was young, good looking, and thanks to his dad, had the kind of connections around Miami that turned the city into something like his playground. Cappy had access to the hottest tickets in town and the interest of the most eligible bachelorettes.

Life was mostly good in the Miami Beach milieu for the son of a well-situated gangster. Take it from Stan Kaplan, who met Cappy at the University of Miami after Kaplan enrolled through the G.I. Bill following his service in the Korean War. The two became fast friends. "Everybody loved Cappy," says Kaplan. "Cappy always had money, always had a nice car. Everybody liked him. He and I hit it off, for whatever reason, and we've remained friends over the years."

In fact, Kaplan is godfather to Cappy's oldest son, Michael, but that event was far off in a future that neither young man would have predicted during their college days. At the University of Miami, Cappy was something of a big man on campus, and Kaplan got a front-row introduction to the colorful side of Miami Beach by riding on Cappy's coattails. "There were all sorts of Damon Runyon characters running around. There were periods of illegal gambling, and the police would cut it out, and it would pop up again. There were all sorts of characters on the beach," says Kaplan. "These guys were from *Guys and Dolls*. It was an incredible era."

Norman "Roughhouse" Rothman, of course, was in the thick of it, says Kaplan. "I don't know how Normie did it. Everybody marveled at it. He got to run the Sans Souci in Havana because it was owned by a family in Pittsburgh, and Normie had some connection with them," says Kaplan, referring to Gabriel "Kelly" Mannarino and his brother Sam. "If Normie had to accomplish a certain thing and he could do it either legally or illegally, he would do it illegally. That was Normie."

Going outside the law may have been acceptable in those circles in those times, but that doesn't mean there were no rules. "The two gatekeepers: the Italian one was Pasquale 'Little Patsy' Erra, and the Jewish gatekeeper was a guy by the name of Maxie Raymond [also known as Maxie Elder and 'Little Maxie']. Maxie held the card room in the Fontainebleau [the most glamorous hotel in Miami Beach]. Patty had a bar/nightclub on Miami Beach called the Dream Bar—great music. Periodically, Maxie and Patsy would meet because somebody wanted to do whatever, and they had to get clearance. And that's how it was on Miami Beach, and peace was kept," explains Kaplan.

Kaplan says it was easy to get swept up in Cappy Rothman's good times. "I remember one night, Cappy said, 'We have to go to the Casablanca Hotel...Let's go and see this new phenomenon called the Twist.' We were going to meet a group of people there. I looked across the table, and there was a woman who looked sort of middle-aged, and she looked rather frumpy. It turned out it was Judy Garland. This was before she went to New York and headlined at the Palace Theater. I said, 'Oh my God, I was drinking with Judy Garland.'"

As for Cappy's pursuit of higher education, Kaplan says, "Cappy was a professional student. When he graduated, he must have had two hundred credits. Somewhere around 1960, he kept switching schools…architecture, business. At one point, he had to take an accounting course for the school of business, and I tutored him because I was an accounting major. It was an unusual situation because Cappy's father had a connection with the Batista people, and they took over a hotel in Miami Beach, the Biltmore Terrace Hotel, and they put on a show from the Tropicana Club from Cuba. They needed someone with a clean record to front the whole operation, so they put Cappy in as the manager of the hotel and the nightclub. So, when I tutored him, I'd go to the hotel and sit in his office and tutor, and he'd get an emergency phone call, and he'd go running off. Sometimes he'd say, 'Come with me,' and we'd wind up backstage, and here were all these Cuban female dancers running around half naked. So that was a great tutoring job for me," laughs Kaplan.

Coincidentally or not, the Twist dance craze actually started in nearby Tampa, Trafficante Jr.'s hometown and stronghold, in 1959, the year Batista fell. At one point, Cappy ran a bar in Miami Beach called the Candy Stix Lounge that became a hot spot for the Twist craze. In other words, the Cuban-flavored party rolled on in Miami even after Castro came to power in Havana. And so did the years Cappy spent as an undergraduate.

By 1959, when Cappy was still muddling his way toward his bachelor's degree, the spillover from Havana landed at his feet. That year, Fulgencio Batista, the freshly exiled former Cuban dictator and friend to the American Mafia, sent his wife, Marta, and his brother-in-law, General Roberto Fernández Miranda, to Florida with $2 million and a mission to buy the Biltmore Terrace Hotel. The rectangular Biltmore Terrace was built on Miami Beach beachfront property at Eighty-Seventh Street and Collins Avenue in 1951. It plugged itself as "the hotel with the wholesome family atmosphere." A who's who of architects had a hand in shaping the hotel's classic Miami modernist style, including Morris Lapidus, who also designed Miami Beach's celebrated Fontainebleau and the Eden Roc hotels.

By purchasing the hotel, Batista's network hoped the fallen leader would live there in exile while plotting his return to power in Cuba—plans for which included paramilitary operations against Castro's regime. Meanwhile, Roughhouse Rothman and Roberto Fernández Miranda got busy outfitting an entire floor of the Biltmore Terrace for Batista and his family to move into, complete with secret elevators.

According to Jack Colhoun's *Gangsterismo: The United States, Cuba and the Mafia, 1933–1966*: "The Biltmore Terrace Hotel operation was pure gangsterismo. Cuban gangster Alberto Ardura [Norman Rothman's good friend and sometime benefactor of Cappy], a close friend of Batista and General Fernandez Miranda, was one of the owners of the Tropicana nightclub. Mafia gambler Norman Rothman was the behind-the-scenes manager of the Biltmore Terrace Hotel."

The Biltmore was also something of a staging for an anti-Castro counter-revolution funded by Batista's inner circle and plotted in collusion with the Miami-area Mafia. Colhoun describes how Cuban gangster Evaristo Garcia, "a very close friend" of Batista, who was tied to the Biltmore Terrace Group and a partner with Santo Trafficante Jr. in several Cuban hotels and casinos, told the FBI that Batista had passed $700,000 to Fernández Miranda to subsidize anti-Castro paramilitary operations. Norman Rothman, writes Colhoun, distributed the funds to Cuban exile commando groups and helped procure weapons and explosives. Colhoun's book alleges that Rothman obtained dynamite for the anti-Castro Cuban Brigade 2456 group to blow up Cuban aircraft at Miami International Airport in August 1958, and also sold one hundred pounds of dynamite to another exile faction to blow up the *Revolución* newspaper in Havana.

Supposedly, Roughhouse Rothman also managed to wrangle something like a small, private air force for pro-Batista guerrillas to carry out bombing raids in Cuba. Colhoun cites FBI reports that implicate the Biltmore Terrace Group with hiring mercenary pilots to fly ten firebombing missions targeting Cuban sugar-cane fields in an attempt to destabilize the economy. Rothman may have also attempted to secure a landing strip in the Yucatán peninsula to use as a base of operations. FBI records, says Colhoun, show that Rothman was integral to purchasing a B-26 aircraft for bombing missions, as well as other small planes. Roughhouse would later be indicted for stealing and conspiring to transport weapons from a National Guard armory.

Colhoun notes other notorious capers involving Rothman, including a plot to put out a hit on William Alexander Morgan, the famous American *comandante* in Castro's revolutionary forces. Morgan had soured on Castro and started aiding anti-Castro insurgents. The idea came from much-feared Batista henchman Rolando Masferrer Rojas, who wanted to collect on the $500,000 bounty put on Morgan's head by Dominican strongman Rafael Trujillo, who believed Morgan had double-crossed him. The opportunistic Rothman was looking for a $100,000 executive fee for organizing the hit. He also managed to get the Mannarino brothers to throw $120,000 into the Biltmore Hotel Group's counter-Castro operations, provided concessions would be granted to them if and when Castro fell.

It seems that the FBI and CIA let a lot of the shenanigans fly in the early days of Castro's rise while the Biltmore Terrace Group plotted the counterrevolution from Miami Beach, and Bastista waited in exile in the Dominican Republic. President Eisenhower, though, eventually refused to allow Batista into the US and didn't endorse his leadership of the Cuban exile community's counterrevolution. Batista ultimately pulled the plug on the Biltmore Terrace Group before his penthouse suite and secret elevator had been completed.[2]

It wasn't long after that Roughhouse caught his first federal charges and convictions for his role in some of those various plots. Among them were violation of the Federal Firearms Act, National Stolen Property Act, and Interstate Transportation of Stolen Property, along with conspiracy charges. In essence, Rothman got caught trying to steal and smuggle munitions, some of them federal property, to anti-Castro forces.

As the charges piled up against his father, Cappy was named secretary of the Biltmore Terrace and the nominal owner of the Bel-Aire Hotel, where he "managed" the Tropicana Lounge at the ripe age of twenty-one. Cappy professes some credulity when it comes to what he was doing and for whom back then but remembers some of the more colorful scenes from that time. Such as getting urgent ship-to-shore calls when he was out on Biscayne Bay entertaining friends on his thirty-two-foot Prowler. He would then have to speed back to the marina and sign papers, never quite sure what he was signing, before going back out on the bay.

Cappy would sometimes act as a bag man for Batista's circle and travel with attaché cases full of money handcuffed to his wrist, passing Cuban currency to exiles in New York, including Batista's wife, Marta, who was ensconced in the Waldorf Astoria. For several years after Batista's fall to Castro, it seemed like the *gangsterismo* simply moved headquarters from Havana to Miami Beach.

While all that intrigue was going on behind the scenes, Cappy stayed away from the fray and mostly took advantage of his connections to sell cigars and perfumes from Cuba out of the trunk of his car. That's about as far into the smuggling racket as he ventured. There was no need to go any further. Cappy was already a charter member of the Miami Beach set, and membership had its privileges.

"We were running a hotel, and we had a wonderful nightclub with a great Cuban revue…That was very successful, and I was the maître d' of that also. So, here I was running a nightclub, having a lounge. I was mostly a host, greeting people as they came in. And [Jimmy] Hoffa came in quite a few times to the show," says Cappy, looking back on his dual existence as a student by day and a Miami Beach impresario by night. "Hoffa always wore white socks…He was always nice to me, probably because of my dad."

When Alberto Ardura was in town, Cappy had access to a twin-engine plane and a learner's flying permit. When a new Chevrolet model called Corvette came roaring onto the scene, Ardura made sure Cappy had one of the first at his disposal, though Cappy says he wasn't a fan; he was too tall, and the car was too small.

Another perk that Cappy had by being part of the Miami Beach set was getting his friends into the magnificent Fontainebleau to see the Rat Pack—Frank Sinatra, Dean Martin, Peter Lawford, Joey Bishop, and Sammy Davis Jr.— whenever they were in town. "I saw the Rat Pack probably a half dozen times when they were at the Fontainebleau," says Cappy. "I remember one time Elvis Presley was in the audience. Another time Judy Garland was there, and she got up, and she was very drunk. Everybody commented about how drunk she was. Peter Lawford was there. They stayed at the Fontainebleau."

Boats, waterskiing, snorkeling, nightlife…life was good, and Cappy was not immune to the allure of his father's friends and their lifestyles, especially when he was young. "Let's just say, I didn't know what I wanted to do, but I liked the position I was in…because he [Roughhouse] had a criminal record, he couldn't get a liquor license, but he could use me, and I would have the liquor license and therefore be involved with the Bel Aire lounge. He really ran it, and I was like the maître d', and I enjoyed having people come in and drink and entertain and just go from table to table and schmooze and get to meet people," says Cappy. "I thought I might follow in his footsteps."

Asked what that meant to him, Cappy says he was intrigued by what appeared to be his father's glamorous lifestyle, and also by the fact that his father seemed to live life on his own terms. "I was certainly impressed with that," Cappy confesses. "I admired him. I thought what he did was very exciting... If I wanted to go to the Fontainebleau and I wanted to go see the Rat Pack, I would say, 'Dad, could you arrange it?' And he would make a phone call and it was taken care of...And good seats, by the way.

"When Beth and I got married, we went to Nassau, and we were treated like we were royalty. When we left, the bill was totally taken care of. My dad was furious when we got home because we had put all of our tips on our bills not knowing that we were going to be comped. When we went to Vegas, whatever we wanted, everything was comped. And we knew to tip with each meal or service! And he [Roughhouse] was well liked—'Let me tell you, son, I think your dad is great'— I got that from everybody," Cappy explains. "He was a bit of a celebrity. When I started to date, like fourteen or fifteen, I was a bit of a hero because my father was considered a gangster, and at the time, gangsters were played by the likes of Humphrey Bogart and Edward G. Robinson and George Raft and Richard Widmark—the mystique of being a gangster was exciting to my peers... When I was older, my dad went to jail, but by then, he was a hero. My friends would envy me. 'God, your dad's in jail, how fantastic! He's a gangster like Humphrey Bogart.' I remember some of the girls, their parents didn't like them dating me because of my dad's background."

Even as Cappy was becoming aware of the darker side of what his father actually did for a living—everything from allegedly running guns to Cuba and arming a guerrilla force, to taking on Castro, to setting up hits, to fencing for a Miami Beach burglary ring and more—he remains mostly uncritical of Roughhouse. "He was the manager and maybe part owner of the Sans Souci Nightclub and Casino, surrounded by important people. Do I think he might have known who killed Kennedy? Maybe. "I was always okay with it, whatever it was. Even now. I'm not going to find out about Kennedy. I'm not going to find out about [Jack] Ruby. I'm not going to find out about Oswald."

It wasn't all rosy, though. Roughhouse could be critical and cutting, but Cappy says that he, unlike so many others, wasn't afraid of him. "I would confront him. You could see him fuming sometimes," says Cappy. "'Your hair is too long,' he'd say, and I would say, 'I like it long'...He was never quite satisfied. If you got a B, he'd say, 'Why didn't you get an A?' If you got an A, he'd say, 'high A or low A?' But when I became a doctor, he was very proud. That was a dynamic change. He told me that if any of his friends say I told them to call you for a favor, don't believe them."

Despite his taste for the trappings of gangster glamour, Cappy was acting as more of a figurehead and a host at the Biltmore and Bel-Aire than a heavy. "I got a salary, but more than the salary, I had a gregarious nature, and I was meeting a lot of people and being invited to parties and affairs," he says. "I was a playboy. I was a good-looking guy, nice car, money in my pocket. Not all the time, it just appeared that way sometimes. But I did pretty good when it came to women."

In most cases, anyway, although his friend Stan Kaplan tells an amusing story of Cappy's first, short-lived marriage to a young woman named Joan Perry. Perry was a girl who performed at the bar of a hotel in Fort Lauderdale, which had a glass window that offered patrons an underwater view of the pool. "She would dive into the pool and do a swimming performance in the window," says Kaplan.

Cappy and Perry met at the University of Miami, where she had been a cheerleader. They were both in their early twenties, and though she was already betrothed to the scion of a wealthy, upstanding family in Fort Lauderdale, the two fell for each other. "She was beautiful," recalls Cappy. "Physically, we got along very well."

Her parents, though, were not pleased with the *Romeo and Juliet* romance and had a habit of, well, kidnapping her from Cappy's clutches, even after they eloped.

At the time, Stan Kaplan was doing the accounting work for the Bel-Aire Hotel, where Norman Rothman ran the bar after the Biltmore Terrace shutdown. "Of course, I knew Normie and I knew people," recalls Stan Kaplan. "Well, I remember when Cappy met this girl from Fort Lauderdale, fell madly in love with her, and eloped. I don't think they [her family] liked having Normie as a relative. I guess I was in law school at that time, 1962 or 1963, and she filed for divorce, and Cappy got his father's criminal attorney to represent him...It was decided that Cappy wouldn't contest the divorce. Back then, it was irreconcilable differences, and you'd have to allege something substantive or substantial to get divorced—like you didn't like the way he squeezed the toothpaste, something stupid. The grounds that she alleged were about Normie's unsavory reputation. Cappy went ballistic and said he would fight it."

The matter dragged on and on until both parties agreed to meet on neutral ground at the Diplomat Hotel in Hollywood, Florida. "We met in the lobby. She was accompanied by this young lawyer, and I accompanied Cappy," says Kaplan.

Then Cappy and his soon-to-be-ex-wife went off to talk in private. "Cappy and his wife came back and said, 'We reconciled, no divorce.' Her lawyer was left standing there with his nose up in the air," Kaplan laughs. "Then one day Cappy calls me and says, 'She's gone again.'" One of the tell-tale signs that she had left was finding a glass animal that she had left behind from her collection.

The on-again-off-again marriage was off for good after a year. Says Cappy, "I think she was as infatuated with me as I was with her. I think if her family didn't kidnap her and take her back—I think that happened twice, maybe even three times—well..."

The marriage was finally annulled, and Cappy would meet his true love, Beth, about five years later.

~

THE GUYS AND DOLLS dream world started to come to an end in the early sixties. Bobby Kennedy's Justice Department and the FBI put the Mafia in its crosshairs, especially in South Florida, where various sheriff's departments had been letting it operate with a wink and a nod and some graft. Rothman was convicted and sentenced to five years for his role in attempting to smuggle guns, money, and munitions into Cuba.

Rothman's FBI file asserts that he was "very close with Santo Trafficante Jr. and the two could be seen together at the Bel-Aire Hotel." Rothman was also believed to be involved with "large jewelry thefts" in the Miami area and fenced the "hot goods" or "ice" as the FBI file puts it. In 1971, Rothman was found guilty on four counts of a fifteen-count indictment for charges related to Interstate Transportation of Stolen Security and sentenced to five years.

It wasn't just federal interference in the old ways of the Mob that was bringing change to the "Magic City." International politics were starting to overtake the parochial pursuits of mobsters and tin-pot dictators alike. The disastrous 1961 Bay of Pigs invasion—which brought together a strange Cold War brew of CIA operatives, Cuban exiles, and Mafia intermediaries for an adventure that in retrospect seemed destined for failure—didn't help.

Cappy, however, was sympathetic to the mission. He'd been horrified by the kangaroo courts and the assassinations of the *Batistianos* who hadn't escaped Cuba or remained behind to fight Castro—some of whom were known around the Rothman household. "It was almost like the Roman Coliseum, but with the Christians going in to a firing squad instead," says Rothman. "There were just horrible things going on at that time."

In fact, he was so riled up that he attempted to join the Bay of Pigs invasion. "Look, I had been ROTC in college. I had been to Ranger training. I was an expert in most of the weaponry of the day. I was young, healthy, had a lot of testosterone running around, and it seemed exciting," says Cappy. "I knew many Cubans, and I was interested in going. But for some reason, I was kept from going. I'm not sure if it was because I was in ROTC or because my father wanted to restrain me, but I know I wasn't able to go with them and, ultimately, I was very happy I wasn't able to go with them."

After the Bay of Pigs debacle, Castro and Soviet Premier Nikita Khrushchev decided to place nuclear ballistic missiles in Cuba to deter any further US meddling on the island. This set the stage for the Cuban Missile Crisis of October 1962… just a few months after Cappy finally graduated from the University of Miami with a degree in marketing, of all things.

When the Cuban Missile Crisis passed and a brief détente between the US and the Soviet Union settled in, the Cold War got hot in Vietnam. US military involvement, which had begun with special-ops and military advisers in the late fifties, escalated to a steady trickle of ground troops not long after Cappy graduated from the University of Miami. That trickle turned into a flood by the mid-sixties. The looming Vietnam War would influence the path the long-meandering Cappy Rothman would take after finally graduating from college.

His first obligation upon graduation, though, was to fulfill his ROTC commitment. The typical commitment then was for six months of active service and eight months in reserve. Cappy, however, had been led to believe that his post-college ROTC orders would be a cushy detail guarding former President Dwight D. Eisenhower while he spent his retirement golfing.

"For four years in the ROTC, I thought I was going to be an MP and that I was going to be assigned to Eisenhower, protecting him when he played golf in Augusta, Georgia. So when I picked up my orders, it said, *two years armored infantry, Vietnam*. I said, 'Where in the hell is Vietnam? Who's going to take care of Eisenhower?'"

Instead of Augusta, Georgia, it appeared that Cappy would be headed to Fort Benning, Georgia, to train as a second lieutenant in the infantry with a possible deployment to a smoldering little conflict on the other side of the world.

Upon getting his orders, Cappy says, he got into an argument with the sergeant at the ROTC office on campus, who told him to accept his orders or be drafted as a grunt. "I said, 'Let me think about it.' He said, 'You can't think about it…we're going to draft you.' I said, 'Give me a few moments,' and I walked out of his office, thought about it for a few moments, got in my car, and drove down to Miami and enlisted in the Coast Guard. As soon as I enlisted in another branch of the service, I was not eligible for the draft," says Cappy. "It changed my entire direction. I'm in the Coast Guard! I don't have to go to Vietnam."

Within a week of enlisting, Cappy was on his way to Cape May, New Jersey, for Coast Guard basic training. Rothman had outgrown his cold urticaria allergy by then, and it was a good thing. He recalls that it was so cold during basic training that the bay the recruits were meant to row in froze over. "All the boats were frozen in the bay," says Cappy. "We couldn't even go rowing."

The experience was remarkable for other reasons, too.

"I was in Papa Company. I was the first Jew a lot of these recruits had seen. They really thought I'd have a tail and webbed feet," says Cappy. "They shaved your hair, got you totally undressed, took your clothing, gave you a uniform, and assigned you to a company. Then they looked up my records and realized I'd already been through Ranger training while in the ROTC and was commissioned Second Lieutenant. They said, 'Well, you're going to be the recruit company commander for Papa Company,' and then the next week, they said, 'Well, you're going to be the recruit regimental commander for the entire cadre of inductees.' So, I was the guy standing up there going, '*Battalions!*'…I had a really wonderful time. I was already well-trained, and as far as helping them out, well,

I could take an M-1 apart, a BAR [Browning Automatic Rifle] apart, a .45 [high-caliber pistol] apart…I was proficient with all of the weapons."

After basic training, recruits matriculate into more focused disciplines for active duty, such as becoming a clerical mate, a boiler tender's mate, machinist's mate, weapons technician, etc. Cappy chose to be a corpsman—basically the equivalent of the Army's field doctor or medic. His reasoning had less to do with a budding interest in medicine than it did with a continuing interest in women. While most of the services back then were still pretty much all male, corpsman training units were composed of "forty sailors, twenty WAVES [women]… and you got to wear civilian clothes," says Cappy. "I said, 'I want to be a corpsman.'"

Following basic training, Cappy was assigned to the famed Naval Hospital Corps School in Great Lakes, Illinois, for twenty-four weeks of medical training. There, something unexpected happened to the playboy from Miami Beach. "I remember it was really, really cold…and I fell in love with medicine!" exclaims Cappy a half a century later, as if it just happened.

It wasn't all love all the time, of course. Cappy not so fondly recalls one incident at sea during a trip between a North Carolina Coast Guard base and Bermuda. The ship got caught in the wake of a hurricane. "Everybody was sick," says Cappy. "I was the corpsman on the trip in case anybody got sick, but I was the sickest. They gave us permission to sleep on the deck because everybody was throwing up in the hull. It was terrible…they served greasy pork chops the first night out, and then a hurricane hit our round-bottom boat…"

Despite that, becoming a corpsman was a revelation. "I loved the science of medicine. I liked the patients. I liked the contact. I liked the diagnostic ability to determine what was wrong and how to help. I graduated with the highest average ever obtained in Corps School. I achieved the highest grade, or one of the highest grades, ever achieved at the time from the Naval Hospital Corps School."

~

THINGS DON'T HAPPEN IN a straight line, of course—especially not big things—and before Cappy started down this new path, he had one more dalliance with the road not taken. It came in the form of Jimmy Hoffa. Norman Rothman's connections and long-term ties had put Cappy in the service of the legendary Teamsters Union leader for several months following Cappy's active Coast Guard corpsman duty.

The Rothmans were familiar with Hoffa and vice versa. Whether Hoffa and Roughhouse went all the way back to Norman Rothman's early union days is unclear, but Cappy says Hoffa was a regular at the Biltmore Terrace Hotel's glamorous lounge. "He liked my dad; that's how I got the job. The union was a little bit different then. I guess there was a little more physicality to it," Cappy says.

Of course, consorting with Jimmy Hoffa could be risky business, and Cappy tells of one incident that stands out when he was still in college. When Rothman was the nominal head of the Biltmore Terrace, one of the gregarious young man's responsibilities was to entertain VIPs for his father and his father's partners. Hoffa was in Miami Beach for some reason, which wasn't unusual, and his entourage decided they wanted to go deep-sea fishing. The Rothmans' thirty-two-foot, twin-engine Prowler was available, and arrangements were made for an outing the morning after a late night at the Biltmore.

The seas were rough that day, and Cappy decided the best way out of Biscayne Bay would be through the Bal Harbor cut of Baker's Haulover inlet at the north end of Miami Beach. But even that typically placid outlet was roiling on this day. "I said, 'We're not going to make it out,'" Cappy recalls, "because you could see the current, and the waves must have been six or seven feet...I didn't want to go out."

As you might imagine, the tough-guy Teamsters, some likely still inebriated, insisted on forging ahead. "This is going to be a tough ride out there," Cappy warned, and sure enough, the boat got rocked in the waves, and one of the Teamsters, Willie, who was leaning against the window, got thrown through the window, smashing his head as he went overboard.

Then the engines cut out, and the boat started taking on water. "I'm trying to keep the boat steady," says Cappy. He yelled at the men still onboard to grab the gaff and try to pull in the man overboard. "They gave him the hook end and held the pole end," Cappy recalls, laughing.

Willie flailed about while the other Teamsters tried unsuccessfully to hook him. Then a wave rose up and tossed Willie back aboard. "He fell right back in the boat," says Cappy.

With the boat dead in the water, the Coast Guard was summoned to save the day. "We had to take [Willie] to the hospital. He had a hundred-some sutures from crashing through the window," says Cappy. "Nobody blamed me because I said I didn't want to do it in the first place." As for the dead boat, nobody cried over that, either. "My dad considered that boat a hole in the water you throw money into," says Cappy.

Norman Rothman's Hoffa connection got Cappy placed in Washington, DC, in the summer of 1963, working for the Teamsters Union's DRIVE initiative. DRIVE is an acronym for Democratic, Republican, Independent Voter Education. It is, in effect, the International Brotherhood of Teamsters' political-action committee. Hoffa set up the PAC in 1959, when the first wave of post–New Deal anti-union politicking began growing into something Hoffa felt he had to combat.

On occasion, Cappy would find himself in Hoffa's office. "Jimmy Hoffa would look out the window of his office—it had a direct view of the Capitol—and he would say, 'That son of a bitch Bobby Kennedy.' And then he'd say, 'Kennedy is probably looking out the window saying the same thing about me.'"

After a while, though, Cappy realized he had a passion that he couldn't deny, despite working in the nation's capital alongside one of the era's most iconic figures. It was a calling ignited at the Naval Hospital Corps School. Finally, he unburdened himself to Hoffa, saying, "I want to go back to school to be a doctor."

According to Cappy, Hoffa looked at him and said, "Great!" Then, Hoffa called Cappy's father to break the news that Cappy was leaving DC. "I went [back to Miami] to pick up my premed courses," says Cappy. "When they saw I had an opportunity to do something other than what they were doing, they encouraged me to take advantage of it…they were very encouraging."

Cappy returned to Miami and enrolled in nearly two years' worth of premed courses at the University of Miami in order to catch up and prepare to apply to med school. In the process, he found an academic dedication and focus he didn't even know he possessed. In early 1965, he applied to the University of Miami Medical School and was waitlisted. According to his old buddy Stan Kaplan, Roughhouse Rothman might have worked some of his magic to tip the scales in Cappy's favor. "Normie knew somebody that he met in prison who put in the good word, and Cappy got in," says Kaplan.

For his own part, Stan Kaplan would go on to law school and become a big-time lawyer in Miami who could count among his clients Maxie Raymond, Paddy Erra, and one of the biggest figures of all in that era: "I probated Meyer Lansky's estate. I'm the trustee of his estate," says Kaplan. "Years ago, I wouldn't talk, but now everybody's dead."

Roughhouse Rothman would be in and out of jail in those days on federal and state charges, or out on bail or parole while contesting charges. He was a master at working the system. "He was very well known by the police," says Cappy. "They liked him. I remember walking into a party with a beautiful Cuban dancer, and these two detectives, who I also knew, got me under the arm and said, 'Your dad doesn't want you here,' and just walked me away, leaving my date left standing there by herself."

Despite how lively Cappy's college years were—not to mention how many of them there were—his life's great adventure started with medical school. So, it's fitting, perhaps, that Norman "Roughhouse" Rothman helped to facilitate Cappy enrolling in medical school—the event that would steer Cappy irrevocably from his father's path.

"Why didn't I go in the same direction as my dad? I fell in love with medicine," says Cappy.

Chapter 5
Calling Dr. Rothman

CAPPY KNEW THAT GETTING into medical school was not going to be an easy task for a self-described C student, who took almost seven years to get his undergraduate degree. So, after returning from his brief tenure in Washington, DC, with Mr. Hoffa, Cappy enrolled in premed courses at the University of Miami, hoping to pick up the credentials he'd need to apply for medical school. He says his days as a South Beach playboy and bon vivant came to an abrupt halt when he began studying in earnest. "My life changed. I had a new direction. I'm trying to think if I was even dating anybody," he laughs.

His new direction started off inauspiciously with quantitative analysis, which was taught by a professor who Cappy describes as arrogant, mean, and an impediment to progress. "It was worse than a boot camp run by Darth Vader," Cappy says. "He prevented many students from continuing. He was so hateful; it seems like his motive was to keep students from becoming doctors…I was so thankful to get a C."

On the bright side, Cappy showed an immediate facility for gross anatomy, the study of visible anatomy (as opposed to microscopic anatomy). This isn't all that surprising considering his boyhood days as an amateur vet. The anatomy class started with dissecting worms and moved on to frogs and then cats. "I used to take the dead cats home. I kept a cat in the refrigerator. I would partially dissect it, and I would finish the dissection on my kitchen table. My mom was cool with it," says Cappy. "I really enjoyed it and was very good at it."

Soon enough, he was studying human anatomy on cadavers donated by the morgue. Cappy was not the least bit squeamish about it. "I enjoyed dissecting. I liked working on anatomy. I would smell of formalin for days just from working on a cadaver. I'm not even sure we wore gloves then. It was fascinating."

Cappy proved to be just as sharp as his scalpel. "I was very good in anatomy. I was asked by the professor to take over the summer class and redissect the cadaver for the students who hadn't passed the course. I almost had a photographic memory," says Cappy, recalling that he could name all 206 bones, 840 muscles, all the arteries, veins, and nerves. "I think human anatomy is fantastic."

While he took premed courses, Cappy picked up extra money and experience working as a pulmonary therapist at nearby Jackson Memorial Hospital, which had a pretty busy emergency room. Cappy made a habit of spending time in the emergency room after his shift. "When I got through working, I'd go down to the ER and just hang around, and by then I knew the guys, and [they knew] I was in premed and had experience through my Corps School training and was knowledgeable."

Before long, the ER staff put Cappy to work dealing with the night's mostly alcohol-related casualties—everything from car accidents to fights. He'd also get sent down to the local holding tank to do some quick patch-up jobs. "They put me in the jail to sew up the drunks," he laughs, amazed at how laissez-faire the whole thing was. "Things were different then. If you could do it, you could do it…I was known as being very good technically."

Cappy's Naval Corps training obviously came in handy while he ramped up for med school, especially the in-depth anatomy and physiology, but Cappy said real-world experience gave him a fresh perspective. "By the time I got out [of Corps School], I knew a lot, I could help a lot, I understood a lot, but I'm not sure I had done a lot."

Despite all that training, and now the real-world, real-time experience he was gaining, medical school was no given. "Medical school had the crème de la crème…the people you are in school with are no slouches," says Cappy. In 1965, the University of Miami accepted one hundred first-year medical students. "I got in as an alternate."

Cappy dug into his studies, living in an apartment near school with no air conditioning and subsisting on Lum's steamed-beer hot dogs and McDonald's. If that sounds like a far cry from his playboy undergraduate lifestyle, in many ways, it was. After getting accepted to med school, Cappy stopped fooling around. He ended up graduating second in his class as a member of the Alpha Omega Alpha Honor Medical Society—basically the medical-school equivalent of Phi Beta Kappa.

Irwin Redlener, who would go on to have a distinguished career as a pediatrician and healthcare-reform activist advocating for underserved children around the world, transferred to the University of Miami Medical School for his final two years. He remembers Cappy well. "He was a very caring and very bright guy," says Redlener. "Cappy and I hit it off immediately."

Redlener, who more recently has become a sought-after commentator and public figure for his many appearances on national news, where his unambiguous and empathetic assessments of the COVID-19 pandemic have earned him many fans, has also been a board member of USA for Africa, and founded the Children's Health Fund with Paul Simon. He is also a disaster-preparedness expert who wrote *Americans at Risk: Why We Are Not Prepared for Megadisasters and What We Can Do*. Redlener has been an advisor to New York Mayor Bill de Blasio, among other things.

At med school, though, the dapper and confident Cappy Rothman showed him the ropes. "Cappy was very generous with his time. People gravitated toward him. He was the good-looking, well-dressed guy in med school. If there was a best-dressed guy, he probably would have gotten it," recalls Redlener. "He stood out in med school, his whole demeanor, his looks, his confidence...He was the kind of person you naturally gravitated toward if you needed something."

Redlener says Cappy was "a very good medical student," but that when the classroom moved into the real world of clinical service, Cappy really shined. "He was quite good at that—quite persistent and attentive to his patients."

Even in med school, Redlener recalls, there was an air about Rothman that heralded things to come. "If I had to bet, I'd say he was going to do something big and different, which certainly manifested itself."

Although the two hadn't kept in touch regularly over the years, Redlener says he recently found himself in need of some help from his old friend. "When I needed help, he was the same Cappy, completely giving, helpful," Redlener says, "The generosity of time and interest and sincerity of his interest... Once a mensch, always a mensch."

∾

IT WAS DURING CAPPY's junior year that he met his future wife, Beth, a stroke of good fortune that changed his course like nothing else to that point in his unorthodox life. This turn of events, though, was quite unexpected and had little to do with his by-now earnest striving toward a career in medicine.

Beth Prostick came from a well-to-do Maplewood, New Jersey, family. When she met Cappy, she was twenty-two, finishing up college and about to start teaching high school English. She played piano and harp and was an alluring combination of brains, bombshell, and junior-league refinement. She also happened to be engaged to a lawyer named Steve from a prominent New York–area family. The wedding was going to be at the Plaza Hotel. It was all going the way it was supposed to go for good girls in those days. Except, that is, for her nagging doubts. "I was engaged but questioning the relationship," Beth confesses.

She met Cappy mostly by accident. Her therapist, whom Beth describes as "practically a clone of Dr. Ruth" and who had met Beth's fiancé, suggested that Beth take her cold feet down to warmer climes. The opportunity came with a trip planned by one of Beth's best friends, Gail, whose identical twin sister had just gotten married. Perhaps feeling a bit left out or left behind, Gail decided she needed a tropical adventure, and Puerto Rico was the place.

Beth's therapist, Lily Ehrlich, urged her to go along. "She said, 'You should go away with the other twin. She's going to need you right now.' And she said, 'By the way, leave your ring at home.' I go, 'Why?' And she said, 'Because you might lose it in the sand.'"

Puerto Rico wasn't quite the panacea the ladies had hoped it would be. "I was miserable," Beth remembers. "I was, like, 'What are we doing here?'" Neither of them had a great answer, other than getting away from New York. Meanwhile, Gail's parents were vacationing in Miami Beach. "I said, 'Well, let's go to Miami Beach and see how that goes.'"

It was 1967, the Summer of Love, when Beth and Gail arrived in Miami Beach. They needed to be shown around, of course. So a mutual friend, Enid Denholtz, called Cappy to let him know that Beth and her friend Gail were in town and needed to be escorted. Cappy quickly called his old buddy from college, Stan Kaplan, who, Cappy says, was always up for an adventure, "no matter what time it was."

Arrangements were made. "The upshot of the whole thing was that my date that night was supposed to be Beth," recalls Kaplan, chuckling. "Somehow, there was a switcheroo and Cappy ended up with Beth."

Apparently, this is news to Beth. "I didn't know I was supposed to be anybody's date," she laughs when told of Kaplan's account. But either way, when Cappy entered the picture, that was it for Beth. "Cappy comes in his velour top, white pants, white shoes, definitely not looking like a Northern, East Coast kind of guy," says Beth, still sounding smitten. "When Enid asked me what I thought of him, I said, 'He's definitely not my type.'"

During the date, Beth tried to act as if she didn't find Cappy at all interesting. She was engaged, after all, but, "By the end of the evening, I was really liking him. There was something so smooth and sincere and warm, and even though he supposedly wasn't my type in his velour, I liked him. I just liked him." Not to mention, she adds, "I was very attracted to him."

Beth spent an extra week in Miami, and when it became apparent that she'd lost her appetite, Gail's mother informed her that it was because she was in love. This was a notion that seemed incredible to Beth even with everything that was going on. She'd already had an engagement party. A wedding date was already set for the Plaza in New York, and her wedding dress had been picked out.

All the plans went out the window, though, when Beth finally admitted to herself why she had doubts about Steve. Beth went home and broke her engagement. "That went over really big with my parents," she deadpans.

Cappy Rothman wasn't such a popular subject back home. "My mom didn't like Cappy," says Beth. "My dad was okay. It was my mom who was not ready for this. My dad was a romantic, so for him, it was, 'Beth's in love, this is great.'"

Her parents, of course, were wary of "Roughhouse" Rothman's reputation, which was known to some of their circle and which Cappy made no attempt to hide. "On the first night I met Cappy, he made it clear that his dad had quite a background. Had been in jail, etcetera," says Beth.

But Beth had done her own background check on Cappy, and their mutual friends were crazy about him. "They thought he was a terrific guy." Also, Lily Ehrlich had also put her seal of approval on Cappy. When Lily knew that she was going to vacation at the Eden Roc in Miami Beach, she told Beth to have that "young man" call her. Cappy, who had no interest in psychiatry, a sub specialty that he had rotated through, made his way to meet Lily at the Eden Roc. Not only did he pass her test, but she added that he would make a really good psychiatrist! Little did she know, psychiatry was the only "C" that Cappy got in medical school.

When people asked Beth about her feelings about Roughhouse, she says, "He was clearly not a man to mess with…I thought he was gruff, but in some ways very principled. There was some aspect of him that [commanded] respect. He was a person to respect, even though he didn't choose the clean path that most of us choose. It bothered me but not very much because I was more interested in Cappy, not what came with him."

Part of what came with Cappy was his playboy reputation, which followed him for some time even after he stopped playing the part. "He was a man. He didn't come across as a grown boy. He was very experienced. When I met him, he'd had those experiences under his belt, and he knew what his path was. He was not in any way a playboy [anymore]," says Beth. "It felt very good to be with some guy who was, you know, really a man."

Cappy, though, wasn't sure how Beth felt. After their quick Miami interlude, she left so abruptly that Cappy was left wondering. "I thought she was gone," he says. He fretted about whether he would hear from her again. He'd thought he'd found a welcome end to his bachelor ways. He was left hanging on the line.

Once Beth recognized why she had doubts about Steve, she returned, without much warning, to New Jersey to terminate her engagement. Once that was done, she had time to think about Cappy and to wonder if she'd ever hear from him again. Beth's father, knowing that his daughter was lovesick, told her to call Cappy and make arrangements to meet up with him— under one condition: he must come to New York. He did, and Beth's parents were satisfied enough to let Beth return to

Miami Beach for another visit with Cappy. The only hiccup was that Beth's mom, the night before the trip, told her that she was accompanying her. "I was mortified as well as horrified," recalls Beth. "In spite of it, I got myself together and never let on to Cappy that I was perturbed that my mother was joining me. It was during this trip that Cappy asked me to marry him."

Cappy was thirty and ready to settle down. In February 1968, Beth and Cappy were married at the Plaza, just six months after they'd met. "The wedding took place at the same hotel as earlier planned, but the dress and the cast of characters were different," jokes Beth.

Oh, and if you were worried about Stan Kaplan getting outmaneuvered by Cappy on that initial outing with Beth, things turned out okay for him, too. He met his wife at Cappy and Beth's wedding. "I've been married for forty-eight years," he adds.

There was, however, one minor snafu at the wedding. The Rothmans were allotted fifty invitations, which may be a lot for a wedding at the super ritzy Plaza Hotel, but it wasn't enough for Norman Rothman. Protocol among his crowd dictated that invitations to his eldest son's wedding needed to go out to all the players as a sign of respect. When told he could only have fifty invites, Rothman simply photocopied the invites and printed his own.

"When I saw that, I got chills. I was like, who am I marrying?" recalls Beth. "I thought, *this is scary*."

Both Beth and Cappy say that Norman Rothman probably didn't expect many of his confreres to show, but when a group of his associates did come, including the Mannarino Brothers, and, according to Rothman's FBI files, Meyer Lansky himself, a table had to be set up and fast. That particular table wouldn't allow any pictures to be taken until near the end of the party when alcohol and good vibes overcame inhibitions. "The only reason it was taken was because Norman or his cohorts arranged it so that they and only they would get a copy of the photograph," says Beth. "My parents never got to see it. Needless to say, they looked for that picture."

The Mannarino brothers and associates weren't the only uninvited guests, either. "Apparently, there were a lot of FBI agents at our wedding," says Cappy.

~

ROTHMAN GRADUATED FROM MEDICAL school in 1969, still practically a newlywed. Following graduation, he embarked on the internships and residencies that get medical practitioners launched into their careers. First stop for Cappy and Beth was Parkland Memorial Hospital in Dallas, Texas. When they arrived, Beth was already pregnant with their first child, Michael. "Cappy wanted a baby immediately," says Beth. "I refused to try until we were married a year."

Michael was born January 5, 1970. And while Cappy was being subjected to the near round-the-clock work hazing that was standard for medical internships in those days, Beth found herself alone in an unfamiliar place. "It was hard. He was working all the time. It was kind of lonely," recalls Beth. "I was a new mother. I didn't know what I was doing. I didn't have any support. I didn't have any friends there. It's Dallas, and there's no coast, which is what I'm familiar with."

The young mother had hoped that Cappy's trajectory would lead them back to the New York area for his surgical residencies after he completed his internship at Parkland Memorial. There, she and her growing family would land on the terra firma of extended family, history, and cultural affinity. All of which were in short supply out West, especially in Texas.

Cappy had other ideas.

"Beth was sure that I was going to practice in the Northeast. So, we're in Dallas, and she has Michael, and she gets a call from Harbor General Hospital [in Torrance, California], which was one of the top residency/internship programs. Parkland was one of the top and Harbor General also; it was a UCLA affiliate," Cappy says. "They said, 'I want to congratulate you. You've been accepted to the surgical residency program.' Beth's response was, 'Oh, this must be a mistake; he never applied.' Harbor General's response was, 'Ma'am, I have his application in front of me.' So when I got back, she was just livid."

Cappy laughs at this memory, and it's easy to do so now, sitting on the deck in a backyard looking out over a Pacific Ocean view framed by palm trees and rolling hillsides. His life is fairly tranquil now, the way it can be when most of life's questions seem to have been settled in your favor, but the journey doesn't always foretell the destination, and there were plenty of trying times for the Rothmans between then and now. And while Cappy may or may not have put in applications to some hospitals in the New York–Boston area, the fact is, Harbor General was one of the best teaching hospitals in the country.

But first, he had to convince Beth to go even farther west. "I said, 'Let's go to California for one year. If you don't like it, we'll go to the Northeast,'" Cappy explains. Beth decided to give it a try. "Well, after living here for one year, we were on a beach looking at the snow-covered mountains to the east and thinking, 'How beautiful,' and by the end of the year, Beth was not wanting to go back." Says Beth, "He thought he would have to convince me to stay out West, but after a year of living in California, I, too, was hooked." It's not surprising that a young couple would want to stay in sunny Southern California, where you can put your toes in the sand all year long, especially when half of that couple was allergic to the cold and spent much of his childhood in Miami Beach and Havana

Harbor General, now known as Harbor-UCLA Medical Center, was originally established by the Army to receive and treat wounded vets returning from the Pacific theater during World War II. Los Angeles County took it over in 1946. The hospital's affiliation with the UCLA School of Medicine began five years later. At Harbor General, Cappy would rotate through neurosurgery, orthopedic surgery, general surgery, plastic surgery, ENT (ear, nose, and throat), and even dental surgery. What he would discover is that he loved surgery and had a talent for it. After all, it wasn't so long ago that he was a premed student taking cats home to dissect on his mother's kitchen table. More surprising, perhaps, is that Cappy discovered he liked urology more than the other rotations he went through.

"I didn't necessarily like the culture of surgery, and I didn't like neurosurgery [brain surgery and back surgery] or general surgery. But I liked urology. There was something about the science of urology, and also, I liked the people I was rotating through urology with," says Cappy. "It seemed to be a group I was compatible with. Doctors whose company I enjoyed more so than in orthopedics or vascular surgery or thoracic surgery…There was something about being in a urological residency—actually it was a rotating residency at Harbor General, so urology was just one of the subspecialties I went through. At that time, they were coming with kidney transplants that I got involved with, and I found it pretty exciting. That's part of urology…In the end, I liked the people in urology better. I especially liked the attending, Dr. Stan Brosman, Chief of Urology at Harbor General Hospital."

Cappy applied for a three-year residency in urology at the prestigious University of California, San Francisco Medical Center. *US News and World Report* ranks UCSF as the fifth-best overall medical center in the US and as the best hospital in California. Clearly, this would be a prestigious assignment for Cappy.

In terms of medical history, though, urology was still a nascent discipline by the time the UCSF Medical Center captured Cappy Rothman's attention, and UCSF was a relative newcomer to the field. Johns Hopkins, Harvard, Columbia, and the University of Pennsylvania all preceded UCSF in establishing urology departments. UCSF, which started a urology division in 1915, made up for lost time under the seminal leadership of the legendary Frank Hinman Sr., the division's first chair.

Hinman helped make UCSF synonymous with modern urology by codifying the practical and philosophical approaches to urology in his foundational 1937 book, *The Principles and Practices of Urology*. UCSF is now ranked number six in urology and number seven in the related specialty of nephrology, the diagnosis and treatment of kidney diseases, particularly in internal medicine and pediatric care.

UCSF accepted Rothman on the condition that he would first complete another year in a general surgical residency or in a specialized residency in nephrology. Since kidney function is one of the primary focuses of urology, Cappy chose to enter a residency in nephrology at the West Los Angeles Veterans Affairs Medical Center on Sawtelle Boulevard. The medical center had evolved from the erstwhile Sawtelle Veterans Home, a care facility for disabled veterans that was built on three hundred acres of former *rancho* land in 1887. The adjacent Los Angeles National Cemetery for veterans followed just a few years later.

For Cappy, the opportunity to further study kidney function fit well with his burgeoning interest in urology. "I think I picked up renal [kidney] medicine as opposed to surgery just to study more of the science of kidney function," Cappy says. "The kidney is a very important organ when you think about its vital functions for life."

Not long after Rothman got to work in West LA, the deadly San Fernando earthquake struck on February 8, 1971. The epicenter was in Sylmar, a town in the northeast San Fernando Valley and home to the San Fernando Veterans Administration Hospital, which was devastated. The construction codes on more than half the forty-six buildings on the onetime tuberculosis hospital's campus predated the 1933 Long Beach earthquake, which ushered in new standards for earthquake-resistant building. At the San Fernando Veterans Administration Hospital, several buildings collapsed during the San Fernando earthquake, and two-thirds of the sixty-four deaths attributed to the quake occurred there. Needless to say, the earthquake stressed resources at the VA's regional medical centers. Cappy was reassigned to the Sepulveda VA Hospital, located then in the North Hills area of the San Fernando Valley.

Rothman, who was working with dialysis patients at the time of the earthquake, ended up running the dialysis unit at the Sepulveda VA Hospital. "That was interesting because we had maybe twenty-four dialysis units—dialysis was relatively new at the time—so if somebody died and a machine became available, we had a list of many applicants who needed a dialysis machine to live," he says. "So we actually sat down with the doctors and attorneys and ethicists—I didn't even know there were ethicists at the time—and the attorneys, clergy, rabbis, social workers, nurses, doctors would go through a pile of like fifty, sixty charts of people that needed renal dialysis to live, and you had to pick one. And I remember the discussions: 'Well, he had two children, he has a good job, this one doesn't have a job, no kids. . .' So you'd actually choose one of the fifty to have this life-saving measure to go on dialysis. That's the state of medicine at the time."

In an eerie and somewhat ironic echo of that era, the almost-as-deadly 1994 Northridge Earthquake later forced the closure of the Sepulveda VA Hospital. Patients and services were absorbed by the West Los Angeles Veterans Administration Hospital, where more than twenty years prior Cappy had started his renal residency.

With this field-tested additional experience under his belt, Cappy finally entered his urology residency at UCSF in 1972. It was then, and still is to a large degree, the house that Frank Hinman Sr. built: a teaching hospital with a research-based approach to clinical practice. It should have been a perfect fit for science-minded Cappy Rothman, and for a time, it was. Especially when he was working closely with Frank Hinman Jr., the senior attending physician in the urology department at UCSF and also the chief of urology at San Francisco General

Hospital. Frank Hinman Sr. trained Hinman Jr., and among Hinman Jr.'s most notable contributions to the field are *The Atlas of Urological Surgery* and *The Atlas of Pediatric Urological Surgery*—not to mention he was one of the founders of the Society of Pediatric Urology.

Hinman Jr. was among the most highly honored practitioners in the field of urology. He specialized in research into bladder defense mechanisms and became a clinical professor at UCSF a decade before Cappy started his residency. He even had a medical condition named after him. Hinman syndrome is a complex continence condition in which children attempt to restrict overly active bladders by tightening the external urethral sphincter muscle, thereby misshaping their bladders into an obstructive state. Hinman Jr.'s research and writing on the subject ended up giving the condition its name.

Like Cappy, Hinman Jr. was a seeker and a Renaissance man. When he wasn't practicing medicine, Hinman Jr. pursued writing and painting. He had a keen sensitivity about the human condition. *Life* magazine published one of his paintings, and two others were used as cover illustrations for *The Journal of the American Medical Association*. Just as important, or perhaps more, he was one of the founders of andrology, at least in its modern incarnation.

Andrology is basically a medical specialty dealing with male health, particularly as it relates to male urological and reproductive issues. It barely existed as a recognized field before Frank Hinman Jr. recruited a cohort of doctors, including Cappy, Anthony Thomas, Larry Lipshultz, Ira Sharlip, and Joe La Nasa, to develop the discipline while Cappy was at UCSF. The revelations that came from Hinman Jr.'s direction had the biggest impacts on Cappy's medical career and life, outside of his wife and kids. It all started with sperm.

For a long time, ironically, the mechanisms of male reproduction were among the least studied subjects in urology. By the time Cappy was getting his feet wet, renal function, the urinary tract, the prostate, and the bladder were the primary concerns, along with vasectomies and vasectomy reversals. Male reproductive health is now a urology subspecialty, but back then, it wasn't given much thought. Kidney transplants were the brave new world of urology and its related field of nephrology.

As Cappy puts it, "The only time the penis became important was if it had cancer because there was not much treatment for impotence, and we all thought it was probably psychological. I think a lot of it is psychological—it just manifests physically. The testicles at that time, we knew they were there, but we didn't know much about how the testicle functioned. The treatment was for cancer, trauma, infection, and congenital abnormalities; not its reproductive function."

Frank Hinman Jr. and his wife, Marion, both had long and rich lives, but they never had children, and Cappy suspects that's where much of Hinman Jr.'s interest in andrology came from. "I think, retrospectively, Frank was probably infertile," Cappy explains. "At his desk, he had a neuroendocrine chart of the gonadotropin cycle—the hormones of the brain that stimulate the testicle. The first year I was there, he gave me the project of answering the question of how sperm got from the testicle to the outside world. So, you'd spend an entire year studying this subject and presenting your findings to the staff. We knew sperm got there [ejaculated], but we didn't know how. The second year, he assigned me the mechanism of erection."

It's hard to grasp now just how fresh a line of inquiry this actually was then. If a guy had erectile dysfunction, people still looked to Freud for answers. And if a couple couldn't conceive, it was assumed to be the woman's fault. When Cappy started looking into these issues in more depth, he was startled by the scant literature and research on the reproductive functions of the testicles and penis.

"At that time, if a guy could have an erection and have an ejaculation, as far as he was concerned, he was fine. There was a certain macho feeling about men—they didn't want to know. But it wasn't always the women's fault," he explains.

Fortunately, Frank Hinman Jr. wanted to know, and Cappy took to the task eagerly.

"It gave me a certain expertise," says Cappy, "and, like I say, I think he was infertile, so I think this was very important. He wanted to learn as much as he could because as urologists at that time, what we learned was what to do if it [the male reproductive organ] had cancer, or if it was traumatized. We learned what to do if it was infected, and we learned what to do if it was congenitally abnormal—if it was undescended, or if it was rotated [torsion]. But we had no idea how it really functioned. We had no idea about sperm production or stimulation."

Most of what was known about sperm production and transportation to the outside world at the time was gleaned from animal husbandry and veterinarian medicine. Cappy dove into researching the mechanisms of erection and ejaculations during his second year of residency at UCSF. One of the things that struck him was how an erection was revered before Christianity and practically reviled afterwards; a shift Cappy credits for much of what ails our culture. "It was the beginning of a period of shame, masochism, and persecution that still prevails. What started out as something beautiful and natural has descended into something more like Dante's vision of hell." (In all of history an erection was considered as a sacred shaft, but after Christianity it was perceived as a demon rod.)

Cappy's rotations eventually led him to the old Southern Pacific Railroad Hospital, which was named Harkness Hospital in Cappy's day. The Southern Pacific Hospital first opened in 1899 as a means of providing medical care for the railroad's workforce. The hospital served railroad workers from all over the West, provided they opted in to the medical coverage with deductions from their paychecks. In that way, the hospital was a precursor to our current healthcare system.

It went through several iterations, but the hospital building constructed after the great earthquake of 1906 became San Francisco's oldest intact hospital. The Southern Pacific Hospital was renamed Harkness in 1968. It closed in 1974, and when it did, Cappy Rothman bought every urology-related resource he could get his hands on—archives, books, nineteenth-century surgical instruments—some dating back to the beginnings of urology.

Things were going well. Cappy was intellectually stimulated and professionally motivated, and he, Beth, and Michael were living in Marin County, just north of San Francisco, in a nice community called Greenbrae. Cappy was enjoying his residency, learning all about urology, and thanks to Frank Hinman Jr., gaining a specialized expertise in male reproductive systems. He was also discovering that he loved studying sperm. "I find it to be the most dynamic cell in the body," says Cappy. "You gotta love sperm. To me, sperm is just one of the most exciting cells in the human body."

Of course, Cappy's appreciation for the male reproductive cell would one day earn him the moniker "the God of Sperm." But that was off on the horizon. In the meantime, there was his work, and there was another preoccupation he needed to make time for: a budding love affair with Yosemite National Park and nature in general. Cappy began making regular forays to Yosemite, hiking the park, and getting good with a camera as well. He also started campaigning with Save the Whales, an organization that was in an urgent global battle to stem the depletion of whale populations largely resulting from the huge commercial whaling practices in countries such as Japan, Norway, the then–Soviet Union, and Peru, among others.

Cappy had also become active in an effort to protest a TV production slated to start filming in Yosemite that would have marred certain landscapes within the park. Oh, and Beth and Cappy had just welcomed their second son, Brett, to the fold during Cappy's first year of his UCSF residency in 1973. "It was very nice for, like, the first two years," Cappy says, almost wistfully of his time at UCSF.

Soon, though, he started bucking against what he perceived to be poor practices and perhaps even ethical lapses at the teaching hospital. "I really became an antagonist against the culture that existed. I really became an advocate for the patients."

Part of the culture, according to Cappy, encouraged performing a significant number of transurethral resections of the prostate, or TURPs, as the procedure is called. The surgery was indicated quite frequently for moderate to severe urinary issues related to a benign enlarged prostate (BPH), which commonly occurs in aging men. To do the procedure, the surgeon would trim away excess prostate tissue that was blocking urine flow. The panoply of medications to treat BPH were not yet available, and the surgery carried some risks back then, particularly bleeding.

Teaching hospitals are arguably more vulnerable to underlying pressures to recommend such learning opportunities as TURPs. "Your experience is very important," explains Cappy, "and this is where you get your experience."

Cappy feared TURPs were being ordered more than what was necessary. One of Cappy's roles as a junior resident was to work up the orders written by the chief resident. The patients were primarily vets or indigents referred by the county since UCSF was not a private hospital. This made them a vulnerable population without a lot of advocates in these situations, especially at that time when doctors' orders were followed with very little pushback.

While working up orders, Rothman noticed what he thought was an overreliance on Sudafed—a pseudoephedrine that constricts the urinary tract—to treat patients complaining of issues with urination. While this may help with incontinence, it also makes it harder to pee. This, in turn, would lead to overordering TURP procedures. Cappy would often recommend the patients take a few days off Sudafed for observation and reevaluation before subjecting them to TURP procedures.

"It was a culture that had grown into: 'How many TURPs did you do?'" says Cappy. "I would work them up, and I would realize what happened, and I would discharge them. And he [the chief resident] would be pissed."

Rothman also took exception to the commonly practiced removal of kidney growths that were more often than not benign. This tended to happen, says Cappy, when x-rays showed a renal mass that was often the result of a cyst, a common occurrence in men over the age of fifty. The standard operating procedure back then was to just remove the mass in case the cyst was cancerous. To find an alternative to what he saw as an overreliance on surgical removal of the cyst, Cappy worked with Peter Julien, who had also graduated from the University of Miami and was also doing his residency at UCSF for radiology. (Julien was later appointed the head of pulmonary radiology at Cedars-Sinai.)

Their opportunity to put their theories to the test came when they had a patient with a renal mass on his x-ray. Instead of going right to surgery, Cappy and Julien drained the cyst, injected dye into the cavity, rolled the patient from one side to the other so that the cyst's margins were clearly visible and then sent the aspirate to pathology. In this way, they could glean enough visual information to determine if the cells were cancerous without subjecting the patient to an open surgery.

According to Rothman, nine times out of ten, the benign cysts required no special treatment. Cappy says that Julien got a hero's welcome when he presented their findings to the radiology department. The surgery-inclined urology department, however, had a different reaction: "I presented it to urology, and I became a persona non grata," says Cappy.

The final straw for Cappy came when he was assisting a senior attending physician who started succumbing to fatigue during a radical prostatectomy. The surgeon decided he would stop during the middle of the procedure and come back the next day to finish. Cappy confronted the surgeon, warning him if he did so, the patient might not be able to urinate again. "By that time, he was just wiped out, and he packed it in," says Cappy. "And I reported him. This was terrible…A good job is a good job, but a terrible job should be reported."

That's when the balance between Cappy and his department reached a tipping point. So much so that the then head of the department, Don Smith, took the unusual step of taking Beth out to lunch. Beth says Smith's purpose was "to see if he could get me to help control Cappy." Smith asked her to get Cappy to be a team player or his days there were numbered. "Cappy wasn't about to play that game," says Beth. "He had a moral conscience, and I couldn't get through to him that his residency was on the line."

Cappy remembers it like this: "I didn't have a problem with Donald Smith. He had a problem with me. I wasn't adhering to the culture. Then he took Beth out to lunch, and he wanted to try to bring me into line, but at that time, I was trying to save the whales and stop the assault on Yosemite."

Rothman was becoming disillusioned with UCSF and perhaps even the culture around surgery; he had started turning to nature and his advocacy for it as a respite.

Cappy's nonconformity and moral conscience, though admirable, made the road a bit bumpy for a new mother with adjustments to make. "It added a lot of pressure," says Beth. "Here I had a new baby, and here we were again in a new place, and Michael was three years old and not exactly a happy camper to have a brother…It was a tough period, and I was, again, being told to not have any needs but also to manipulate Cappy to listen [to the senior members of UCSF's urology department]."

Cappy, of course, did not conform, and matters came to a head. "My dynamics with this group were not working out, and [they] determined that I was not compatible with the culture there," says Cappy. "I thought what I was doing was appropriate…I guess I was not necessarily a team player."

The good news was that UCSF had a deal with Loma Linda University Medical School Center in Loma Linda, California, near Redlands in San Bernardino County. Loma Linda needed a board-certified urologist—a relatively new standard that was required of urology departments in order to keep their California certifications. Although Cappy left UCSF, he finished his third year and final year of residency at Loma Linda.

Cappy fit in well with the urology department at Loma Linda. "I was the token non–Seventh Day Adventist," he says, referring to Loma Linda University's religious roots.

Rothman may have been the token among the Seventh Day Adventists—many of whom don't eat meat, drink coffee, season their food with pepper, etc.—but being so had its advantages. For instance, the department liked to go out to dinner at the local steakhouse, even though they were not permitted to eat meat. "They were vegetarians. So, I'd give one resident my potato, and he'd give me his steak," Cappy recalls, laughing. "They were a wonderful group to work with. I liked that group of guys."

He also got to do a lot of surgery—kidneys, adrenal glands, bladder stones, TURPs, just about everything that came with the territory. "But these surgeries were indicated to help the patients—not train the doctors," he says.

"I went to Loma Linda and did very well." Cappy also did well for Loma Linda. He scored in the ninety-eighth percentile with the second highest score on the urology boards in the country. "Loma Linda never had a board-certified resident urologist," says Cappy. "They gave me a way to finish my residency and get board certified, and I gave them a certified resident urologist…I put them on the map."

Then, almost as soon as Cappy had completed his residency, he got the call that would bring him one step closer to being "the God of Sperm."

Chapter 6

Into Andrology

THE CALL CAME FROM none other than Frank Hinman Jr., who hadn't forgotten Cappy, nor the research Cappy had done while he was a resident at UCSF under Hinman's direction.

It was late 1975, and Hinman was aware that Rothman's residency at Loma Linda was coming to an end. Hinman had his own hopes for Cappy's career direction. Rothman had begun to develop a keen interest in the emerging technologies of endoscopic surgery while under the tutelage of Roger Barnes, the legendary head of the Loma Linda urology department. In fact, Cappy was seriously considering endoscopy as a potential specialty, and, in 1979, he would publish a paper with Barnes on the cause, prevention, and treatment of scar tissue that sometimes develops in the bladder neck following prostate surgery.

Hinman Jr., though, was the man who sparked Rothman's interest in sperm by assigning him two yearlong research projects during his UCSF residency: "How Does Sperm Get From the Testicle to the Outside World?" and "The Mechanism of an Erection." When he got wind that Ed Tyler, the founder of the nationally acclaimed infertility clinic in Westwood, was looking for a urologist to take charge of a new and barely known area of fertility—andrology—he suggested Rothman.

Hinman Jr., as you'll recall, never had children, and Cappy suspected he had a personal stake in male-factor infertility. He started recruiting—or "seeding," as Cappy puts it—a handful of young urologists into fertility clinics and practices around the country: Larry Lipshultz, who now heads the urology and male-reproductive divisions of the Urology Department at Baylor College of Medicine in Houston, Texas, but who was then running the male-infertility clinic within the division of urology at the University of Philadelphia; Joe A. La Nasa, in Louisiana; Anthony Thomas, in Cleveland; and Ira Sharlip, with whom Cappy had been a resident at UCSF.

Rothman was Hinman's man in Los Angeles. "We were the beginning of a new wave of doctors that was interested in the other half of the fertility issue—sperm and men. We started to contribute the other twenty-three chromosomes," says Cappy. "He [Hinman Jr.] kind of appointed us to develop the field of andrology."

Cappy is quick to point out that even Hinman Jr.'s dream team of future andrologists was standing on the shoulders of giants such as Dr. Lawrence Dubin and Dr. Richard Amelar, who were among the first to recognize the need for the sort of medical discipline that would later develop into the field of andrology. According to the Society for the Study of Male Reproduction, Dubin and Amelar are known for, among other things, the Dubin-Amelar varicocele classification—a clinical assessment of varicocele severity based on physical examination. In 2002, the Society of Reproductive Medicine awarded Dubin—who passed in 2018 at the age of eighty-four—the Distinguished Service Award.

Dubin was himself inspired by Dr. Charles W. Charny, a charter member of the American Fertility Society in 1944, when infertility among couples was almost exclusively considered to be a female issue. *The New York Times*, in its 1992 obituary of Charny, credits him with being among the first to recognize the importance of varicoceles (dilated veins in the scrotum that overheat sperm) in male infertility and for bringing pioneering surgical techniques to treat varicoceles back to the United States from England. According to the *Times*, "Charny was joined by another urologist, Dr. Robert Hotchkiss of New York University, and a biologist, Dr. John MacLeod of Cornell University Medical School, in affirming male infertility as a subspecialty of urology."

Andrology took that affirmation of male infertility and made it not just a subspecialty of urology, but its own field. Hinman's dream team, Cappy Rothman among them, became the avant-garde. "It was just serendipitous that Frank Hinman assigned me 'How Does Sperm Get From the Testicle to the Outside World' and 'The Mechanism of Erection.' And then I was hired by Ed Tyler at the Tyler Clinic," says Cappy. "As soon as I got here, I was needed. They didn't need another urologist in Los Angeles, but to have somebody specializing in this small, esoteric field of infertility was needed."

Soon after Hinman made the call to Ed Tyler, Cappy accepted Tyler's invitation to join him at the clinic he founded in West Los Angeles in 1950. According to *The New York Times*, Tyler and his clinic innovated many of the standard treatments and practices for infertility, including establishing the first private sperm bank in the country. Tyler also introduced "the pill" to Southern California in the early sixties and was among the first private clinicians to use the fertility drugs Clomid and Pergonal, a follicle-stimulating hormone that increases ovulation. Tyler, a director of the American Fertility Society and president of the Pacific Coast Fertility Society from 1960 to 1961, was integral to legitimizing the treatment of infertility as private medical practice. Talk about a growth industry.

Tyler, who overcame his own fertility issues, was known as an optimist and someone who was bullish about medical intervention in the process of conception. Dangling on the edge of hucksterism, Tyler made direct appeals to women over forty seeking children, stating unconditionally that his clinic would not turn them away. Sometimes the Tyler Clinic came under fire, such as in 1985, when a woman under the clinic's care gave birth to septuplets.

It's safe to say that Cappy learned not just the clinical aspects of fertility treatment and sperm banking at the Tyler Clinic, but also the attitude that his job was to provide a service for people who were sometimes in desperate straits when it comes to the primal imperative to start a family. During his nearly two years at the Tyler Clinic, Cappy Rothman became the first doctor in Los Angeles specializing in the male side of infertility.

Says Cappy: "I got fascinated with the whole field—constantly amazed at how well sperm worked, most of the time, and how often we could intercede when it didn't. Thinking about where we are now is just amazing. When I started, we did not even have intrauterine insemination, and the most you could do was intracervical insemination. But then it went to intrauterine insemination, and then it went to IVF...I was there in the beginning of IVF with [Patrick] Steptoe and all of the people from Australia and England that were developing it and going to the conferences and meeting them...It was exciting, developing the field and developing within the field."

One of the early investigators, Pierre Soupart, MD, was a professor of obstetrics and gynecology at Vanderbilt University and a celebrated biochemist and expert on fertilization mechanisms. He published numerous articles on the future of successful human in vitro fertilization, the technique used to produce the test tube baby. In the late 1970s, there were many significant advances in reproductive biology. Cappy recalls having dinner with Pierre at the Fountainbleau Hotel in Miami Beach during an ASRM meeting. Pierre shared that he had fused two rat eggs that had developed into a viable embryo. Not only was this unheard of, but for Cappy it was reminiscent of *Brave New World* in which males were no longer needed for procreation. During dinner, Pierre left to call his lab and when he returned, he shared that the experiment was ruined because the mother rat had consumed the fetus. Pierre, unfortunately, died in 1981; a great loss to reproductive biology.

What made developing a clinical practice in andrology so exciting for Rothman was how new and unexplored it all was. There would be plenty of room to contribute, and any advances in the field would be breakthroughs by definition.

"When I started, there was no andrology. People didn't even know the word. All you see is basically female gynecology and fertility," he says. "When I started practice at the Tyler Clinic, I would see a couple, and the woman would have two operative procedures to determine why she was not pregnant before a man even had a sperm count to determine if he was sterile. It always seemed to be a woman's issue. If a man could get an erection and ejaculate, there was a whole psychology that it wasn't a man's problem."

The profound bias in the field of fertility in those days showed itself in obvious and not-so-obvious ways. The most obvious, of course, was that medicine overwhelmingly viewed infertility as a woman's problem, not a couples' issue and certainly not a man's. There were many subtle manifestations of this bias, too, such as women using birth control pills for years, thereby stressing their bodies with unnecessary hormones, while their husbands were actually infertile the whole time. Men were simply not put under the microscope, so to speak.

In a short time, male infertility went from barely being considered an issue to being acknowledged as responsible for about fifty percent of infertility issues among couples. This may seem obvious now, but it wasn't as recently as the early 1970s. "I felt like I was walking into a cave with a match, and basically, if I didn't fall and hurt myself, other people might be interested," says Cappy. "Now we have floodlights in this cave. There is so much information coming into it."

Andrology also enabled Cappy to make good use of his budding specialty—sperm. During the 1980s, Cappy's interest in sperm continued to fascinate him, and he became absorbed with the question of sperm morphology and evolution. He started researching the incredible diversity in sperm as Darwin did with his *The Origin of Species*. He started with the classification of animals, not plants, and realized it was an enormous undertaking. While attending a meeting on spermatology in Siena, Italy, he met many scientists and doctors with like interests.

Cappy started to review the published available literature. Some authors had compiled a book on insect sperm alone. Realizing that this task was overwhelming, Cappy decided to continue by limiting his studies to mammals only. His friend and colleague, John Critser, Ph.D., a brilliant and well-known cryobiologist with multiple publications on the subject of sperm preservation, was of the same mind as Cappy. John was planning an African safari to collect as many animals' sperm for cryopreservation. Cappy assisted by financing him with the caveat of receiving photos and electron microscopy images of various mammalian species. After reviewing the photo micrographs and the information he received, Cappy was no closer to his goal of developing an evolutionary tree from insect to human sperm. John, unfortunately, died in 2011 at the age of fifty-seven. This project is still ongoing, but Cappy does not think it will be accomplished in his lifetime. Even though there are many researchers and scientists attempting this enormous task, a direct evolutionary line will probably never be achieved. The collection and cryopreservation of sperm of various mammals that were nearing extinction was a plus that came out of John and Cappy's work.

"If one has to study one cell on the body, I cannot think of a more interesting cell to study than the sperm," says Rothman. "A sperm is one cell. It takes about three months to develop in the testicle. And once it's ejaculated, it has a choice—remember, over one hundred million sperm are ejaculated, and only one sperm gets to the egg. So the distance of a sperm traveling from the cervix to the egg is comparable to you or myself running from Los Angeles to Seattle. And it makes it in minutes…It's the only cell that has motility like that.

"It was a fascinating field. It is a dynamic cell to study. Just looking under the microscope to see them whizzing around, and all the different shapes and different cellular matter. I would put samples away for a week and study them every day."

Advances in technology enabled Cappy to take a closer look at sperm than had previously been possible and see the cells up close and in action. "What I did when I started my practice is I actually videotaped the sperm samples because it's so subjective—you can't count hundreds of millions of sperm cells, but you can extrapolate from one drop and the volume, what the entire sperm count should be. But to try and be more precise, I was actually videoing it. Every time I saw a patient in follow-up, I would make a three-minute video, as well as a formal semen analysis."

Soon enough, Cappy went from "going to lectures about infertility to giving them." And there were plenty of questions to address in the burgeoning field, especially as assisted conception started to take off. Why does nature pair one female egg with the millions of sperm cells in male ejaculate? Why do only a hundred to a thousand of the millions of sperm get through the cervix? How does only one sperm penetrate the egg to fertilize it? Is natural selection involved in picking the right sperm? With the ability to see sperm better and with the increasing understanding of the male role in infertility, could doctors wade into the provenance of nature and select the right sperm themselves?

Cappy collaborated with Dr. Luciano Zamboni, a pathologist at UCLA-Harbor Medical Center, who would go on to become an UCLA emeritus professor of pathology and laboratory medicine. "A colorful character and a great cook," according to Cappy, Zamboni also pioneered using electron microscopy to study the microanatomy of sperm cells in order to take a closer look at things like shape and form. The electron microscopy brought a much clearer picture, literally and figuratively, to our understanding of sperm cell physiology and pathology—what is now known as morphology.

Morphology is a relatively new factor in assessing fertility. It used to be that if a man had a high enough sperm count and the sperm had decent motility, he was considered fertile. As technology enabled doctors like Zamboni and Rothman to examine sperm cells more closely, they began to see how irregularities in physiology and molecular makeup affect male fertility.

By incrementally applying technologies that initially were not developed with fertility procedures in mind—Cappy frequently borrowed microscopic equipment from ENTs in the early days of his microsurgical practice—doctors focusing on sperm helped pave the way for watershed moments that were soon to follow, such as the first in vitro fertilization in 1978 and, later, IVF via intracytoplasmic sperm injection, or ICSI, by which a single sperm is injected directly into the egg.

In the early days of Cappy's career, these advances were "like a chapter in *Brave New World*," he says. "The thought of being able to inject a sperm into an egg without hurting it…and then being able to take cells from blastomeres (a dividing cell from a fertilized zygote) to check for genetic disease carriers… We are really accelerating the process.

"Now, we are trying to pick the right sperm from a man who has fertility problems, some of which may be genetic, some of which may be environmental, but we're able to take a poor quality [semen sample] and select a sperm and inject it into an egg," says Cappy. "We're bypassing a lot of the natural barriers without significant ramifications, and it seems like the children born through IVF are not different than the children born naturally. So, how important is this selective process of nature?"

In an unfortunate twist of fate, Ed Tyler died just three weeks after sealing the deal to bring Cappy onboard. Rothman, though, must have made quite an impression on Tyler and his family because Tyler's surviving wife and children asked Cappy to do his eulogy. After Ed Tyler passed, the Tyler Clinic came under the authority of Dr. Jaroslav "Jay" Marik and Dr. Stanley Friedman, Tyler's codirectors, almost as soon as Cappy arrived.

For a while, things went along just fine.

Cappy was learning the techniques of sperm banking while also learning more and more about the intricacies of male infertility. He became a believer in sperm banks not just as an insurance policy for men who underwent vasectomies or who were undergoing cancer treatments that might put their fertility at risk, but also as places to store donor sperm—a fertility treatment that was barely acknowledged at the time, though donor sperm had been used to impregnate women for centuries, usually on the sly.

At the same time, Cappy was doing groundbreaking research on the body's immunological responses to vasectomies and vasectomy reversals. "Sperm develop in a unique environment. The body doesn't know that sperm are there because a blood–testis barrier—an impenetrable barrier that protects sperm from the body—surrounds the cells. When you are born, there are no sperm. As you develop and go through puberty, as sperm develop, new proteins and new antigens grow within this barrier that the body doesn't recognize. If the body realizes sperm are present, it will create antibodies that attack sperm."

What Cappy found was that open-ended vasectomies were often leading to an inflammatory response because sperm proteins were not fully ensconced behind the blood–testis barrier, and the body was attacking sperm. Furthermore, it was sometimes difficult to conceive following vasectomy reversals because the sperm would agglutinate due to the antibodies.

It was this research that led to Rothman parting ways with the Tyler Clinic. Cappy had been presenting his research at American Urological Association conferences for more than a year and had prepared a talk on his findings for the annual conference of the American Society of Reproductive Medicine in late 1976. It was a subject he'd been giving presentations on for a year by then, starting with "Immunological Aspects of Vasovasostomy," which Rothman presented at a conference for the Western Section of the American Urological Association in San Diego in 1975. He gave a similar talk at a symposium at the Beverly Hills Hilton Hotel in October of the following year.

In the months leading up to the annual ASRM gathering, though, Rothman's father, who had recently been released from federal prison, fell ill. Cappy went to Florida to attend to his father. In his absence, he asked Dr. Stanley Friedman to deliver the talk. Friedman gave the talk and then published Cappy's research about three months later. "I saw my paper in the *Journal of Andrologia*—'Immunological Aspects of Vasovasostomy,' by Stan Friedman. I was never mentioned," says Cappy, more incredulous than bitter. "My paper."

Cappy confronted Friedman and was told that any work published from his clinic belonged to him and the clinic. "I left the clinic that day," says Cappy.

When he left, he took a burgeoning expertise and interest in sperm banking with him. "I learned about sperm banking in 1975 while working at the Tyler Clinic. I cared for many couples who wanted children, but the man was either infertile or sterile," explains Cappy. Too often, he says, he'd find himself sitting across the desk from a couple, and the sad, angry wife would say, "Because I married you, I will never be a mother."

There were few options for these cases at the time. Adoption was difficult, and IVF and intracytoplasmic sperm injection (ICSI) were still a few years away. An alternative, not widely used at the time, but one for which Cappy saw many opportunities to relieve suffering and bring joy, was to use donor sperm for cases in which male infertility was the primary issue with conception. "I initially offered this service to my patients and gradually to the gynecologists within the Los Angeles area. I didn't think of it as a business at the time— just as a service to couples who were hurting because they thought they couldn't have children," says Rothman.

Soon, the service spread throughout California and then to every state in the country and eventually to forty countries, making the California Cryobank the largest sperm bank in the world. It was a long road, however, from walking out of the Tyler Clinic to becoming "The God of Sperm."

Chapter 7

Start With the Semen

WHEN CAPPY ROTHMAN LEFT the Tyler Clinic in 1976, he didn't have any inkling that he would eventually be the subject of dozens of newspaper and magazine articles, and appear frequently on local and national television, including *The Oprah Winfrey Show*, *60 Minutes*, *The Morning Show*, *20/20*, *Donohue*, just to name a few.

At the time, he was mostly concerned with developing his own medical practice and providing for his wife, Beth, and their two sons, Michael, then six years old, and Brett, three. Despite the clichés about wealthy physicians, Cappy was like a lot of doctors when they are starting out—not exactly struggling but not living the high life, either.

Los Angeles wasn't a renter-friendly city even then, and Cappy and Beth struggled to find a place for their growing family. "Most landlords would accept pets, but they wouldn't accept children," Cappy recalls. This was the dilemma in 1970, when they first moved to Los Angeles and lived in an apartment in the Fox Hills neighborhood of Culver City. Fox Hills wasn't the toniest address on the Westside. It was a relatively new development, best known for its proximity to the just-opened Fox Hills Mall and for attracting young professionals on the rise with its abundance of apartments and condominiums.

In 1975, when Cappy took the position at the Tyler Clinic and needed to move from Riverside to Los Angeles, the family rented a home on Enchanted Way in Pacific Palisades. Having finished his residencies and multiple moves, this seemed like the start of Cappy and Beth's "enchanted" future.

Cappy's post–Tyler Clinic private practice started just as modestly—in an office at 2080 Century Park East, Suite 907, where Marty Rosenblatt, a renowned nephrologist and family friend ("a third cousin twice removed," Cappy jokes) let Cappy share his space. The office location worked well since Cappy was affiliated with Century City Hospital, located next door, and also had hospital privileges at Cedars-Sinai and UCLA Medical. Sharing space with Rosenblatt presented some incompatibilities: his patients, both male and female, were mainly older with renal disease. Cappy's patients were mainly young males whose fertility needed evaluation. A sperm count was a necessary part of the work-up. The patients were told to use the office's restroom in order to give an ejaculate. *Playboy* magazines were used to help the process. It was not surprising to wonder what Marty's patients thought if they came across the magazines while using the restroom.

Within two years of sharing office space, Rosenblatt wanted to bring in an associate and moved to a larger office. At that time, the office became Cappy's, and he was able to remodel it the way he wanted. Unlike most medical offices, the waiting room had a custom-made puzzle table where patients could gather around and put puzzles together. There was also a Pac Man table in the office. There were kaleidoscopes in every room that the patients could busy themselves with. Cappy, as well as his staff, dressed casually. The office had no formality, and the intent was to disarm patients who most likely were stressed from the stigma of infertility or any of the procedures such as vasectomies, vasectomy reversals, and varicocelectomies. Rothman even had a shirt that was decorated with sperm that he wore while performing vasectomies!

The staff recalls some funny moments. One had to do with Rothman calling for "Ruth," his lab tech, who replied "I'm coming." Rothman had to take her back to his office and say "We don't say I'm coming in this office!" Another had to do with one of the staff asking if the patient brought in his sperm sample. He nodded and handed her his sample in a baggy; not even a zip-lock bag. This was certainly not the jar that she expected, but she maintained a straight face after accepting it. There was another time that Cappy accepted a donor he had given an extensive work-up to. Three of the women working in the office said, "You can accept him, but we'll never use him. He's ugly." And so, that became another criteria for accepting a donor!

Rothman would soon start making a name for himself as an adroit surgeon, especially when it came to vasectomies and vasectomy reversals, a fairly delicate procedure. Cappy's ambidexterity, enforced way back in grade school when he simply wasn't allowed to be left-handed, proved to be a difference maker in these procedures.

Despite the demand for vasectomies and vasectomy reversals, Cappy maintained a general urological practice, taking on patients with urinary-tract infections, and men who had blood in their urine, testicular cancer, and a wide range of issues. While his decision to focus on andrology and sperm banking may seem like a natural progression from his brief time with Hinman Jr. and Ed Tyler, it wasn't exactly fated. In fact, it was a sudden visit by his old friend Stephen "Bud" Sacks that cast the die. Cappy had roomed with Sacks while the two took their urology board exams.

Sacks happened to drop by for a visit just as Rothman was looking over the file of a female patient who had been referred to him after blood started showing up in her urine. Cappy worked her up and discovered she had renal-cell carcinoma, a type of kidney cancer. He took the opportunity of Sacks' visit to show him the x-rays.

"Hey, Cappy, when was the last time you did a nephrectomy?" Sacks asked him.

Cappy replied that it had been maybe a year or more.

"Well, I did four in the last six months," Sacks replied.

The implications were not lost on Rothman. "I took the X-rays off the box," he says, "gave the chart to Bud, called up the patient, and said, 'I have a great doctor for you!' And I realized, 'I'm not going to do urology anymore. I'm just going to do male infertility.'"

Cappy soon became the main man in this nascent field. "I wasn't a threat to the urologists in the community, so everybody was referring [patients] to me," he explains. "If anything happened with male infertility, I was the go-to guy."

And a lot was starting to happen in male infertility.

First and foremost, there was the growing understanding that male infertility existed. Until the early 1970s, if a couple was having trouble conceiving, responsibility was laid at the woman's feet. But the women's liberation movement coincided with the civil rights movement in this country, and by the mid-seventies, those ideas had started to find their way into sexual and reproductive politics.

"When I started to practice, women were often subjected to two or three exploratory procedures before the man was checked out," Rothman explains. Evolving social mores led to men slowly taking more responsibility for fertility, as well as birth control. As a result, vasectomies grew in popularity as the tail end of the postwar baby boom intersected with the women's movement—though, to be clear, vasectomy still lags far behind female sterilization as a birth control option.

A vasectomy is a simple surgical procedure by which the two vas deferens ducts are severed and tied so that sperm stored in the epididymis will not be able to reach the urethra. It's the male form of tubal ligation. Though vasectomies are cheaper, faster, safer, and more effective than female sterilization, in the US, twenty-seven percent of sexually active women have had a tubal ligation, while just nine percent of men have had a vasectomy. Men in developed countries such as New Zealand and Canada get more vasectomies than here, though that might also be a function of how healthcare coverage works in those countries.

The popularity of the procedure has declined somewhat in recent years, but even so, some 500,000 vasectomies are performed in the US every year.[3] Though they are meant to be permanent, vasectomies are reversible and, no surprise, with the rise in vasectomies came an inevitable increase in the demand to have the sterilization procedure reversed, especially as divorce rates and second marriages increased. A reversal, the vasovasostomy surgery, is a much more delicate procedure than a vasectomy, as the integrity of the vas deferens—vulnerable to scar tissue and infection—must be maintained after reconnecting the tubes.

An anomaly of the postwar baby boom is that by the end of it, we began to see male sperm counts decline noticeably. Or at least the conventional thinking goes that since 1973, when reliable data on the subject of male fertility and sperm counts started being tracked, men have undergone a fifty percent decline in sperm count throughout the West—North America, Europe, Australia, and New Zealand. Normal sperm counts have gone from ninety-nine million sperm per milliliter of semen to forty-seven million (still well within the range of fertility), dropping one percent per year with no sign of leveling off—leading some epidemiologists to warn that we could be entering a *Handmaid's Tale* type of reproductive dystopia.[4]

Leading andrologists who analyze sperm on a daily basis are often skeptical of this data and remain less convinced the end of male reproductive capacity is correct. Cappy is one who doubts that there has been a significant drop in sperm count or efficacy and says his experience has shown him that even the best sperm analysis should be considered to have a twenty percent variable.

"I think it's variable, but I don't think there's been a decline in sperm count. I think if you wanted to get attention and hype you'd start with this, but I don't think it's correct," he argues. "My fifty years of looking at sperm does not discern any decrease in males' sperm counts. The way we look at sperm is so subjective and inherently inaccurate. You're taking one drop from a sperm sample and looking at it under a microscope and extrapolating. If you took a different drop, you'd get a different reading."

Nonetheless, these trends boded well for a guy who was on the cutting edge of studying, storing, and analyzing sperm—not to mention highly adept at vasovasostomy surgery. Rothman came into his own riding a building wave of new attention to male reproductive health. Andrology, in effect, became the male analogy to gynecology.

"I liked it, and I was open about it, and I was a strong advocate of it. I tried to inform that if you're going to work up an infertile couple, one of the first things you should do is get a semen analysis on the guy," says Cappy. "The doctors at the time would work up a woman before they'd even do a semen analysis on the guy. I'd say, 'No, start with the semen! If a couple comes in, and if the woman is not obviously hirsute or obese or other indications, just get a sperm count on the guy, and you'll know.' That was like discovering a new world."

While hormones and medications were being used on women to improve their fertility, Rothman thought out of the box and tried using female hormones on men, as well as Clomid, Pergonal, and HCG. He found this to be effective.

∿

AT FIRST, THE SPERM bank was just a sidebar, a service Cappy learned at the Tyler Clinic under Ed Tyler's tutelage. When Cappy left the Tyler Clinic, he took his know-how and a liquid-nitrogen storage tank for freezing and saving sperm samples with him. Initially, Rothman was most concerned with saving the sperm of patients who were going into the military or those he was treating for testicular cancer. The majority of the men whose sperm he stored were patients for whom Cappy was about to perform a vasectomy.

Storing sperm for vasectomy patients wasn't fashionable at that time. Urologists generally viewed vasectomies as a permanent procedure. If an individual wanted to store sperm before having a vasectomy, they reasoned, he shouldn't get one. Cappy disagreed. "Vasectomy was the easiest, simplest, least expensive, most effective form of birth control at the time," Rothman explains. "But the urologists would not mention sperm banking because they thought if a patient wanted to bank sperm, he was ambivalent about his decision. That's not the way it goes. People change, circumstances change. I was recommending that guys having vasectomies put some sperm away, because I was doing so many vasectomy reversals, it just made sense. Put sperm in the sperm bank before you have a vasectomy, and if at any time you change your mind, we use those sperm."

At this time, Cappy was primarily a surgeon—one who was quickly gaining a reputation as the steadiest hand in town when it came to vasectomy, vasovasostomy, varicocelectomy, testicular cancer, and semen analysis. "I was booked up for months," says Cappy. "You couldn't get to see me. My surgery was scheduled five days a week for six months."

Cappy's reputation was enhanced by his early adoption of the newest microsurgical technologies, which turned out to be particularly well matched to his ambidexterity.

Earl Owen, an Australian-born contemporary of Rothman's, was a strong influence. Owen was a classically-trained pianist growing up in Sydney in a family of doctors. During his childhood, Owen was plagued by medical problems stemming from a tumor on his leg. The radiation treatments weakened his bones, causing them to break often. Owen had to undergo many surgeries, and he came to hate the cumbersome approaches to surgery.

Owen graduated from the University of Sydney Medical School, and in his medical practice, pioneered microsurgery. He is credited with performing the first microsurgery vasectomy reversals and tubal ligations. But he really made his mark by successfully reattaching the finger of a young boy who had accidentally chopped it off with an ax.

Just attempting this procedure shocked the world, and it wasn't popular with Owen's bosses at the Royal Alexandra Hospital for Children in Sydney. To do it, Owen sewed the finger's severed nerve endings together by using a needle under a microscope. Against most expectations, the surgery was successful. For his efforts, Owen was fired for insubordination— no doubt cementing his esteem in Rothman's eyes. Owen would go on to do hand transplants, and eventually trained the French surgeons who performed the first face transplant in 2005 on a woman who had been attacked by her own dog.

Owen, who died in 2014, also had an interest in ergonomics—he would contribute seating designs to the Sydney Opera House—and worked with Michael Patkin, the Australian surgeon who pioneered applying ergonomics to surgical procedures. These two did a lot to bring surgical techniques out of the nineteenth-century "sawbones" culture and into the modern world of technological innovation. Cappy invited and hosted them for a week in Los Angeles, at Century City Hospital, discussing improvements for microsurgery in the operating room. Rothman had always been open to new ideas, and this was no exception. "I got fascinated with microsurgery," says Cappy.

The only problem was that, in the US, microsurgery was not being taught in any of the surgical subspecialties—and especially not in urology. So Cappy pilfered ideas, techniques, and even equipment from ophthalmologists, ENTs—anyone who was using advanced techniques and equipment. "I would watch the ophthalmologists and the ENT doctors work, and learn techniques from them," Cappy explains. "Remember, there were no specialized instruments for urologists, no sutures for urologists, but just going to the eye doctor's locker—'Hey, I could use this. I could use that.' And the hospital [Century City] was very accommodating."

The hospital might not have been so accommodating if it realized the lengths to which Cappy was going to perfect his microsurgery skills. "I would go to the pet store, and I would buy a couple of rats and bring them up to the operating room, and I would just whack their heads against the table to knock them out," says Cappy, "and I would operate on rats just so I would have viable tissue, so that if I made a mistake, it would bleed."

After he got comfortable enough working on rats, the next step was to simulate doing sensitive operations on human tissue. Luckily, Cappy had developed a relationship with the chief of pathology at Century City, a doctor named Charles Sims, who had also been a resident at Loma Linda prior to Cappy's arrival. Charles, known as Chuck, and Cappy would eventually form a highly consequential partnership, but for now, Cappy simply needed spare parts. "I would ask Chuck, because he was in pathology, 'What do you have?' And he would give me part of a kidney, part of a liver. I would take human organs upstairs, and I would operate on them."

As Sims explains it, leftover surgical and autopsy specimens were typically held for months or years after the pathology department had made a diagnosis before the tissue was disposed of by a biological-waste service. "I found some surgery specimens and autopsy specimens Cappy would practice on," says Sims. "In those days, the pathologist had a lot of leeway...He [Cappy] would be given permission to practice on the organs."

Cappy says he was driven by the understanding, much as Earl Owen was as a child, that the surgical practices being employed in urology and now andrology were mismatched to the task at hand. It was like bringing a saw to a sewing circle. "People were doing vasovasostomies, but they were doing gross surgery with minimal success," says Rothman. "I said, 'I can do better than that.' The incentive was that patients needed it."

Sims agrees that Rothman was singularly focused. "He was driven to excel," Sims explains. "He wasn't satisfied with being okay. He would go to any step he could to be the best. He was easily the best in the department at microsurgery. He could finish a surgery faster and more efficiently than any other urologist in the department. He didn't have any wasted moves. He was an outstanding microsurgeon, particularly in doing vasovasostomy surgeries and restoring fertility [to men]."

Microsurgery soon became one of Rothman's specialties, and before too long, he was working with Michael Patkin, the ergonomist, and consulting with Earl Owen to remodel operating rooms at Century City to better accommodate microsurgery. Cappy started lecturing on ergonomics, and in the ensuing years, would travel to Japan to study the most advanced microscopic and laser-surgical technology, video, and instrumentation. In order to discover what was most efficient, Cappy would video himself with a stopwatch to improve his technique. He also hired and trained his own first assistant to work with him in surgery. Adding to his quest for efficiency, he used the laser to fuse the ends of the vas. This had not been done before.

All this new technology and technique must have seemed like a fine dose of kismet for Cappy, whose ambidexterity was paying off in ways he couldn't have foreseen all those years ago. "I felt so comfortable and liked it so much. It's a delicate procedure. It's difficult to work under the microscope, but I could use my right hand as easily as my left," he says.

This combination enabled Rothman to do, as he puts it, "exactly what I wanted, rather than what was easy. I really got a reputation for microsurgery, and I loved it. I could do a bilateral vasovasostomy with three-layer closure in under an hour and a half. I even did it under local in my office for guys who couldn't afford to go to the hospital…I used the ophthalmologist's microscope."

The net effect was that Rothman was in high demand rather quickly after going into private practice. "And I stayed that way for thirty-five years. I was busier than I could be. When it came to microsurgery, I was probably one of the best in the world. People would come to watch me operate and say I had a license to steal," says Rothman. "I did more reverse vasectomies than probably anybody, except maybe Earl Owen."

Being in high demand also led to Cappy's having a celebrity practice. He enjoyed seeing leading directors, famous actors, composers, singers, and more. These experiences were part of the perks of his practice. Word once got out that a leading male celebrity came to his office, and it was written up in *People Magazine*. Women came to the waiting room in hopes of sitting in the chair that the celebrity sat in.

~

BEING BOOKED IN ADVANCE for six months of surgeries was a good scheduling problem. Even as his surgical practice was booming, Cappy continued to bank sperm for patients as a component of his andrology practice. In an office separate from his own that he rented from a radiologist on the third floor of Century City Hospital, Rothman would store sperm, mostly, for patients undergoing vasectomies and those with testicular cancer.

Delving further into andrology, though, he started to notice another need: to help couples who wanted children but discovered that the male partner was infertile. Keep in mind, this was the mid-seventies, and as we've said, urology hadn't yet caught up to male-infertility issues, at least not to the degree Cappy had. Rothman was soon getting more and more referrals from other urologists who lacked his deep knowledge of sperm and who hadn't invested the time to learn microsurgery and other technologies Cappy was putting to use. The combination of his research background and

Cappy with his parents in 1938

Cappy and his mother,
Ethel "Eddye" Rothman in 1938

Cappy sitting on top of his father's car in 1938

*Cappy's father, Norman "Roughhouse" Rothman with Elvis Presley
at the Dream Lounge in Miami Beach.*

Sans Souci Cabaret nighclub and casino in Havana, Cuba.

Left to right: Norman; Billy Eckstine; Patsy Erra, godfather of Miami Beach; and friend

The Line-Up: (Left to right) Santos Trafficante respectfully refusing to answer questions; Norman "Roughhouse" Roth-man at his 1960 gun smuggling trial; Castro hit-squad organizer Johnny Roselli, whose body turned up in a Miami bay two months after he testified before the Senate; and his boss, Sam Giancana, who took seven bullets in the face a week before his scheduled testimony

Left to right: Santos Trafficante, Norman Rothman, Johnny Roselli, Sam Giancana

Cappy with a spear gun at the age of sixteen
in Miami Beach

Cappy and his mother at
Valley Forge Military Academy

Cappy with Rimrock at Valley Forge. Riding was a saving grace
for Cappy during his time at military school.

Beth and Cappy at their wedding in 1968   *Beth and Cappy on their honeymoon in Jamaica*

Beth on the beach in Sam, a 1967 Pontiac Bonneville

Beth and Cappy during their hippie stage in Los Angeles, 1972

Beth holding their first son, Michael,
when he was one year old

The Rothman family:
Beth, Michael, Brett, Jason, and Cappy

Beth and Cappy summiting Mount Whitney

This photograph taken by Cappy from the top of Half Dome at Yosemite.

Cappy graduating from the Univerity of Miami School of Medicine in 1969

Cappy at Jackson Memorial Medical Hospital while a student.

This photograph of Cappy in his office, taken by Douglas Kirland, was featured in the NY Times Magazine in 1980.

Cappy standing outside Bourne Hall in Cambridge, where he trained under Patrick Steptoe—the first doctor to do in vitro fertilization

Residency by Cappy in the school of Architecture, 1995

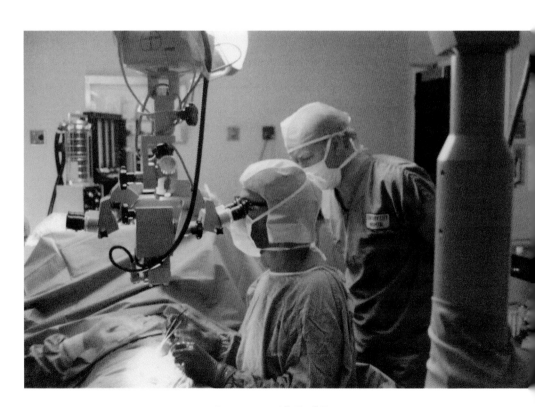

In surgery with Earl Owen

Cappy in Shanghai for the opening of the Chinese sperm bank

Earl Owen and Cappy in 1977

Patrick Steptoe (center, on crutches) was the guest of honor at the unveiling of the third IVF center in the US, opened by Cappy (on Patrick's left) and Mark Surrey (on Patrick's right).

Cappy in his lab, featuring pictures of children born successfully at his practice

Cappy and Phillip Li at the California Cryobank in 1989.
Cappy would go on to be a consultant for sperm banking in China

Cappy and Morley in 2000

California Cryobank booth at ESHRE: European Society of Human Reproduction and Embryology
Left to right: Kaj Rydman, Scott Brown, CEO Pamela Richardson, and Cappy

Cappy having a laugh at ESHRE

The BBC documentary Donor Unknown *won first prize at the Tribecca Film Festival. Cappy was featured in the documentary and answered questions at the festival itself. The two women pictured are children of Donor Unknown.*

Cappy in is office, featuring a mobile from Star Trek's Deep Space Nine, *a set of movie prop wheels, and a penis bone from a walrus (on the desk).*

Cappy with his three sons: Jason, Micheal, Brett

Cappy and Beth in their home in 2020

Top Left: Cappy Rothman and Dani Shapiro, author of Inheritance
Top Right: Irwin Redlener and Cappy Rothman

Errol Flynn, Norman Rothman, and friends at the San Souci

Cappy Rothman on top of Half Dome

The Rothmans, 2024

technological savvy gave Rothman a decided advantage in semen analysis. He was able to show patients their own sperm on video and explain the sperm's properties—the motility and morphology of their samples.

Cappy's interest in male-factor infertility predated IVF and came at a time when adoption wasn't an easy route for couples to take, either. For couples having trouble conceiving, even intrauterine insemination (using a device to put semen inside the uterus) was considered advanced and not widely practiced at this juncture. The most popular intervention was to put sperm in a cervical cup, put it up against the cervix, and "cross your fingers. There were not many other options," says Cappy.

~

GIVEN THE NUMBER OF couples seeking some alternative to adoption, Cappy thought there ought to be more ways to help them. So, he started storing donor sperm as an option for clients being referred to him with male-fertility issues. "It wasn't one couple, it was many couples," Cappy recalls. "The guy is devastated. He did not ever think he was going to be infertile. He realized, under duress, that something needed to be done, and he accepted a sperm donor because they couldn't adopt and he could just feel the pain of his wife."

This was the beginning of the California Cryobank, the largest and most sophisticated sperm bank and repository of reproductive and genetic material in the world, one that would eventually store enough genetic material to repopulate the world more than once.

To get an idea of its scale: The California Cryobank sends upwards of 34,000 ampoules of sperm to clients around the world every year, each ampoule containing at least sixty million sperm cells. "Someday I might be portrayed as a villain," Rothman half-jokes, "because right now, I'm responsible for the birth of about 230,000 children. You take that, bring it out three generations, and you're probably talking about millions of people. That's a significant population that the California Cryobank is responsible for."

These days, potential California Cryobank sperm donors must go through sophisticated genetic screenings, as well as health and psychological workups. Cappy is fond of saying that it's easier to get into Harvard Law School than it is to be accepted as a California Cryobank sperm donor. In the early days, though, it was a little more freewheeling, especially when it came to picking the "right" donor.

Back then, it was all kept mum, and that's pretty much been the practice until recently. Donors were anonymous, and couples preferred that the process remain confidential as well. Most children from the first generation of donor pregnancies, says Cappy, didn't even know their dads were not their biological fathers. "We didn't even have genetics back then. We didn't even have computers then. We tried as best we could to match the physical characteristics of the donor to the physical characteristics of the husband, which is why we had to have the diversity of donors," Cappy explains. "We would have questions like 'What's your favorite color, movie, etc.?' to get some idea about the donor. We found out the husband would usually not want to hear anything. He wanted very little to do with picking out the donor."

Though the husbands were often uncomfortable with the prospect of using donor sperm, Rothman says, "They would have felt more uncomfortable if we didn't have donor insemination…It was a service that was really necessary. It preceded IVF. This was just offered as an option, and I'd say most of the [infertile] couples did in fact take it, and I started to get very busy."

Chapter 8

Fire

SPRING 1978 WAS A hopeful time for Cappy Rothman and family. The California Cryobank was starting to grow, and Rothman's private practice was blooming. Signifying their good fortunes, the family moved into a modest ranch house on a hillside in tony Pacific Palisades at the very western edge of Los Angeles. The house provided ocean views through a frame of lush eucalyptus groves and pine trees.

The house cost $200,000, a small fortune at the time. The Rothmans borrowed the money to make a down payment. "Beth's folks from the East Coast thought we were crazy; they thought we were buying a mansion, buying a city," Cappy remembers. "We wanted a deck and view. That excluded most of the places east of here."

Even though a comparable house in that neighborhood would go for about twenty times that these days, and even though the house was a bit of a fixer-upper, it was a major commitment for the Rothmans, whose kids, Michael and Brett, would turn eight and five that year.

Meanwhile, on the other side of the country, the US House of Representatives Select Committee on Assassinations deposed Norman "Roughhouse" Rothman on April 16, 1978. The deposition concerned CIA and Mafia entanglements in various attempts to take out Castro after he took power, along with the CIA and Mob's entanglements in similar misadventures. In a coincidence that may be illustrative of the different paths father and son were on, the Select Committee deposed Rothman in Miami the same month and year that Cappy Rothman published his first major article, "Clinical Aspects of Sperm Banking."

Roughhouse had been released by the US Department of Justice Bureau of Prisons three years earlier, in October 1975, after serving his time in a federal penitentiary in Atlanta, Georgia, for a number of charges related to interstate transportation of stolen securities. Rothman's official parole review cites his failing health from severe degenerative osteoarthritis and a cervical-spine condition. It notes that there was no therapy for his condition. Norman "Roughhouse" Rothman, once an imposing figure at 5'11" and 215 pounds, was a stooped-over man dealing with chronic pain in his neck who looked older than his sixty years at the time he was paroled to his residence in Surfside, a suburb of Miami Beach.

That didn't mean he was no longer a person of interest to those investigating the long reach of the Mafia in America. According to House Select Committee hearing documents, the CIA had been tracking Rothman since 1958, when Roughhouse had absconded to Dallas after the fall of Havana. Rothman was known to the CIA as "a hoodlum with ties to pre-Castro Cuba" with "a long history of gambling, illegal arms dealing, theft, and other shady activities." The CIA noted his indictment for theft and transportation of firearms, as well as his involvement in the Canadian securities caper that resulted in his second federal indictment (the gun-running charges in 1959 being the first) in the early sixties.

The FBI files on Rothman didn't paint a rosier picture. They document a man who was an admitted friend and associate of Paddy Erra, Santos Trafficante Jr., Sammy and Gabriel "Kelly" Mannarino, and other notorious mobsters. The FBI believed Rothman was running a large jewelry theft and fencing ring around Miami, banking *bolita* and other sporting bets, laundering hot securities, and engaging in a variety of other "shady" activities. The files mention that Meyer Lansky was seen at Cappy Rothman's wedding reception in 1968, along with "other big shot hoodlums from the Miami area."

The House Select Committee investigating the Mafia found good reason to depose Rothman and did on several occasions. The committee's report is the stuff of Kennedy and Castro conspiracy fever dreams, referencing Lansky, Trafficante Jr., and other notables from the era. Rothman gets his own subchapter in the report: "The committee investigated Norman Rothman, who was active in the operation of various casinos in Cuba before the Castro takeover and who consequently maintained associations with organized crime and the Batista regime."

The report cites FBI files on Norman Rothman indicating that, according to Rothman at least, a quid pro quo was on the table: Castro's assassination in exchange for no prison time for his 1960 gun-running conviction. Rothman said he'd been in contact with high-ranking members of the Kennedy administration, including White House lawyer Harry Hall Wilson and Assistant Attorney General John Seigenthaler. Rothman is quoted in the deposition as saying he was summoned on more than one occasion to Attorney General Robert Kennedy's office to discuss providing contacts inside Cuba.

"One of them happened to discuss [the assassination of Castro] with me, but not in a technical way. You know, just in a casual way. That is about it. I cannot for the moment remember it word for word because it is too far back," Rothman is reported telling the committee.

He "expected to avoid imprisonment," according to the report, should he prevail in orchestrating the hit on Castro. The report then goes on to call Rothman's assertions of meetings with Kennedy's Justice Department "uncorroborated" and "highly unlikely" given Robert Kennedy's crackdown on organized crime. But a common purpose, such as getting rid of Castro, can make strange bedfellows.

That Cappy's first major publication (excepting, of course, "Immunological Aspects of Vasovasostomy," which Stan Friedman, then of the Tyler Clinic, had published in 1976 without crediting Cappy) would come out the same month his father was being grilled by a House subcommittee illustrates the whiplash-inducing dissonance between the fates of father and son. "Clinical Aspects of Sperm Banking" was written for *The American Journal of Urology* and published in April 1978.

Cappy had done quite a bit of lecturing on the subject by then, and the paper codified and modernized the best practices for a procedure that had been around in some form or another for decades but hadn't really been formalized by the medical community. That changed with Cappy. He was a refreshing presence in the staid world of medical professionals, with his velvet pants, open-neck shirts, and shaggy hair. He seemed like a man of the times, injecting a sorely needed dose of modernity into what seemed like an anachronistic profession. "I was unique. What I was doing was unique. I was really the only urologist in Los Angeles that was focusing just on male infertility," says Cappy. "I was lecturing somewhere once a week, or maybe twice a week because it was an exciting field."

As for his penchant for velvet pants, Rothman laughs while explaining, "They felt good, and they looked good. For the next ten years, I only had velvet pants, all different colors—green, brown, black, beige…It almost became like a signature."

Sperm banking—cryogenically freezing one's sperm for future use—was considered such a novelty at the time that Phil Donahue interviewed Rothman on his popular daytime TV show twice, and *The New York Times Magazine* published an article on the subject featuring Cappy. The novelty of cryogenically freezing sperm, however, was soon replaced in the public imagination by another, even more shocking advance in reproductive medicine. On July 25, 1978, Britain's Patrick Steptoe and Robert Edwards used in vitro fertilization

(IVF) to help Lesley Brown conceive the first so-called test-tube baby, Louise Joy Brown, ushering in a new era of reproductive possibilities.

After a long, hot summer that year in Los Angeles came autumn, which brought LA's notorious hot and dry Santa Ana winds. They had been blowing for days by October 23, 1978, and the gusts were reaching speeds of up to fifty mph as they moved east to west, tearing through the canyons of West Los Angeles, turning the area into a tinderbox. That day, a power line went down on Mulholland Drive near the Skirball Center, setting off a fast-moving wildfire that stretched from Agoura Hills at the western reaches of the San Fernando Valley to Malibu on the other side of the Santa Monica Mountains.

Three separate fires broke out within twelve hours, moving quickly and stretching the resources of firefighters, whose communications were blocked by the mountainous terrain the fires were consuming rapaciously. That may be one of the reasons residents in Cappy's new neighborhood say they were late in getting the word to evacuate. "We never had any notification that we were going to have a fire," says Rothman. "There were no police, no fire department, nothing on the radio. Basically, as far as we knew, it was all smoke and no fire."

His wife, though, throughout the day could see the brown air and feel the heat of the fire building. Beth called Cappy and begged him to come home. Cappy, who was wrapped up at work, didn't believe that they were in imminent danger. To appease Beth, Cappy checked with the fire department and was told that the fire wasn't coming their way. Beth decided otherwise, and her friend Patty Coppola, who was at the Rothmans' house with her two children, helped Beth grab whatever they could and put it in the trunk of her car. "Can be replaced, can't be replaced" became Beth's mantra.

Meanwhile, Beth called a friend of Cappy's and had him relay the message that he needed to get home fast. "I got home, and I could see the smoke rising from over the hill," says Cappy.

As soon as Cappy arrived at home, Beth remembers, she looked out from their front yard and yelled, "There's a fire, I can see it. Flames are pouring down the mountain." Cappy still wasn't ready to leave, though. He didn't at first grasp the gravity of the situation and was prepared to fight the fire with a garden hose if it came down the hill to their property. "It was the only idea I had. I'd never met anybody who lost their home in a fire," says Cappy.

The winds were wild and hard to predict. There was no good way of knowing whether the fire would descend the hill or cut north or south. In fact, Cappy says, he learned that a neighbor across the street was able to save half his home by dousing embers with hoses. "I wanted to stay with the house," Cappy recalls, "but Beth said no way and that she and the kids weren't going to leave without me. It was pretty traumatic."

When Cappy saw the fire cresting the mountains to the north of them, just a stone's throw away, he decided it was time to go. It was too late by then for him to grab many of his things. "It was a matter of heat, smoke, ash…It was pretty terrifying," he says.

Cappy, Beth, Michael, and Brett got out with what they could manage to put in the trunks of their cars—clothes and necessities. Beth took her great grandmother's candlesticks and family photos. "Unfortunately, she took some of my clothes, which were nothing to save," says Cappy, "and lost her wardrobe of really couture clothing, including some Emilio Pucci dresses. Because her family was into fashion, she had some magnificent clothing."

The Rothmans also lost a growing art collection that included work that focused on the horrors of the Nazi invasion of Russia from the point of view of a Russian Catholic who emigrated to the US. "We had a lot of great art that we lost," says Cappy. "We lost everything."

For Michael and Brett, two little boys who lost their home in the fire, they were afraid that the fire could happen again. Brett asked, "What will we do if there's another fire?" Beth reassured him by telling him that there was no brush to burn and we would, therefore, be okay. But Brett had another question, "But we don't have a burglar alarm. What if someone breaks in?" Keeping it simple for a five year old, Beth told him that there was nothing left to steal and there was no need to worry.

Among the most devastating losses for Cappy were the antiquities he had salvaged from the old Harkness Hospital in San Francisco, where Rothman worked as a resident before it closed down in 1974. The collection had medical books, instruments, and paraphernalia dating back to the 1700s. In the end, the Mandeville Fire destroyed 230 homes and damaged dozens more. Three people died during the blazes, and fifty were injured. More than twenty-two homes in the Rothmans' neighborhood were lost, including theirs.

Decades later, sitting on the deck of the beautiful home that he and Beth built, literally, on the ashes of their old residence—with its modest pool, koi pond, and stunning views of the shimmering Pacific—Cappy reflects on the experience. "When I look back, our house could have been nicknamed "potential inferno," because it was surrounded by pine trees, juniper… but it was beautiful. It was the first house we'd ever owned. As a matter of fact, we'd owned it for just six months. We had just got done fixing it up. We lost it six months after we bought it. It was just so foreign to me that I would lose my house to a fire in Los Angeles."

The evacuation from the fire was chaotic with the roads down the canyons in the Palisades narrow and winding. "At one point, it seemed like we were going to have to abandon our car in order to get out. It was terrifying," says Beth. The Rothmans went to Malibu to stay with their friends, Patty and Art Coppola. On the drive to their house, it looked like they were driving into a fire storm and wondered if the fire would turn them away. What they didn't realize was two fires were happening on the same day: the Mandeville Fire and the Agoura Fire that stretched from Agoura to the Broad Beach. To Beth, it felt like Armageddon.

That first night, after the danger had passed, Cappy made his way back up the canyons to Las Lomas Avenue, where his house should have been. The house next to his was burned to the ground, as was the house right across the street. "I was able to sneak back up here at night, through the barriers, and I could see that we'd lost everything," Rothman says. "I felt totally empty—shock, anger, concern, wondering where your future goes…to the very end, the fire department said, 'You have nothing to worry about,' even when I was on the phone saying, 'I'm looking at it [the fire].' They were totally inefficient, non-communicative, overwhelmed."

Some eighty-one fire trucks and engines were called to fight the three fires that burned more than 38,000 acres in Mandeville Canyon, Agoura Hills, and the mountains north of Pasadena. In postmortems done on the firefighting response, the general consensus was that it could have been worse given how quickly the fires sparked and spread, and how unpredictable the intense Santa Ana winds made the fire's paths.

There was also some acknowledgment that the mutual-aid agreements that call in fire departments from the entire state to help were slow in comparison to the fire's ferocity and that radio contact among various companies was lost at times in the hilly terrain. Some Pacific Palisades residents complained about the lack of resources dedicated to them—how the departments didn't want to venture up the area's "spaghetti streets."

"You have to make value judgments," John Gerard, the Los Angeles city fire chief at the time, told the press. "It's one of the toughest things I've had to do. I really can't think of anything we should have done differently."

Cappy disagreed. At one community meeting in the aftermath of the fire, Rothman remembers, he took over the podium—uninvited—from Councilman Marvin Braude. "I said, 'He wasn't there. I was there. I know what happened.' And I basically nudged him off the podium and took over, telling people what took place…I was angry," explains Rothman. "I'd lost my house in LA. I'd lost my house in a fire, and nobody had warned us."

Beth Rothman remembers the night of the fire vividly. Safe at their friends' home in Malibu, she decided to go for a swim. She had a revelation. "That night I swam in their pool, and I never felt such freedom," says Beth. "Freedom knowing that I had my family, that we're all alive, and I don't need anything… You forget it. You forget it along the way, but in the moment— and it lasted more than a moment—there is a deep knowledge of what's important."

When they were allowed to return to the lot, only a fireplace was left standing. "There was no semblance of anything. It struck me," says Beth. "The erasibility of time was just incredibly vivid. Something you don't really want to look at. Without a moment's notice, it's gone as if it never existed."

The City ended up paying out $8.5 million to insurance agencies and homeowners whose homes were damaged. For his part, the fires politicized Cappy. "He felt the fire department let him down," says Beth. "He was outraged."

His primary target became a massive home development proposed for the ridge above the Rothmans' house, the very ridge the fire had traveled down to get to Cappy's house. The land had belonged to Deanna Durbin, the star actress and singer from the old studio-system days of Hollywood. At first, says Rothman, it was intended to be a golf course, but then developer Ray Watt was able to get the parcel rezoned residential and subdivided.

Watt had initially proposed somewhere between five hundred and one thousand homes for the subdivision above the Rothmans' house. To Cappy, this seemed insane given what had just happened. "I was saying, 'You can't build up there because we were trapped here. How could you possibly build up there?'"

Rothman was able to stir up grassroots community opposition to the project, so much so that the mayor's office took notice. "Because I was so articulate—well, maybe not so articulate, but so vocal and so annoying, in people's faces—Mayor Tom Bradley actually assigned one of his aides, Steve Saltzman, to be a liaison with me," says Rothman.

Cappy earned the nickname Don Quixote for his attempts to defeat the real-estate development in a city where, at the time, it was nearly impossible. Beth thinks the moniker was apt. "He was like Don Quixote when it came to trying to stop this development up above," she says. "He was fighting City Hall, literally."

Though Cappy held off development for a while, a scaled-down version of the project eventually went through. "I was able to stop them from building for a period of time—I had the media; I had the press. I was on radio. I wrote articles. I was interviewed frequently by the *Los Angeles Times*."

That the final development ended up significantly more modest than the one proposed was small consolation to Rothman. "Ultimately, I think he built about 150 homes up there. I'm not even sure. He never had any intention of building a thousand homes," says Cappy. "I didn't realize how affluent Ray Watt was compared to me, and how he had more support because he had more money." Cappy did get an inkling of Watt's power when he learned that Watt asked Dave Wilstein, the owner of the medical building, to evict him. Fortunately, Dave liked Cappy and did not go along with the plan. But the fire officials that originally agreed that there would not be sufficient emergency egress for the community above, that the access street was so steep that garbage trucks had to go up in reverse, changed their stance and voted to accept the development. Someone, namely Ray Watt, got to them.

Watt died in 2009 and, according to a *Los Angeles Times* obituary, "was a pioneer and innovator in the development industry who continually created new products to meet the tastes of Southern California as the region grew after World War II. He was widely credited as the first in the West to popularize condominiums, strip shopping centers, time-share vacation homes, and residential communities with shared amenities such as golf courses, tennis courts, swimming pools, and lakes."[5]

When asked what he took away from the experience, Rothman says, "I learned how corrupt people think corruptly."

Chapter 9

Ice

CAPPY SAYS THE FIRE was "a reality check," the first time "something unexpected and existential" happened to him. The fire was, indeed, a momentous event, one that will always mark that year in Cappy's mind, but 1978 would have stacked up as exceptional anyway.

That year had begun busily enough for Rothman. In February, he gave a presentation titled "Male Infertility" to postgraduates at Loma Linda University. That same month, he did a talk on "Practical Management of the Infertile Couple" at the Edward Tyler Symposium at the Las Vegas Hilton. In April, Rothman presented "A New Approach to the Infertile Couple" at the Valley Presbyterian Hospital Urological Conference in Los Angeles.

This flurry of activity was in keeping with the growing demand for Rothman as a speaker and go-to expert in the relatively new field of reproductive medicine, especially as it applied to male fertility, or andrology as it was just starting to be called. At the Western Section of the American Urological Association Conference, held in Seattle in late summer 1978, Rothman participated in panels on semen analysis—one titled "Medical Therapy of the Subfertile Male"—and others on artificial insemination and sperm banking.

He continued advocating for the technology and techniques of microsurgery at the World Microsurgery Congress II in San Francisco that September. By the fall, Rothman had started working the topic of sperm banking into his public speaking more and more. In fact, just weeks after the fire, he gave a talk on "Treatment of Male Infertility With Special Emphasis on Sperm Banking" at St. John's Hospital in Santa Monica.

These subjects may seem like no big deal now, but it's hard to overstate how new, exciting, and disconcerting the ideas about freezing and storing one's genetic material for future use by someone who will most likely have no connection to the sperm's source were to many at the time.

Indeed, these days, when Louise Joy Brown is in her forties with children of her own, we tend to take even IVF for granted. Such was not the case in 1978, nor would it be for years to come. In fact, Patrick Steptoe and Robert Edwards were treated like Dr. Frankenstein when the news of Louise Brown's birth broke.

"It was viewed with absolute suspicion," Professor Peter Braude, head of the Department of Women's Heath at King's College London, told the *The Guardian* in a 2013 article marking Louise Brown's thirty-fifth birthday. "If you talk to people today about human reproductive cloning, the feeling you get that it is playing God is just how it was in 1978 with IVF."[6]

Less than a year after Louise Joy Brown came into the world, the second IVF baby was born in England with a boy named Alastair. Australia joined in a year later, and then the first IVF baby was born in the US in 1981. By then, the entire population of children conceived by fertilizing eggs outside the human body stood at fifteen.

In the early days of IVF, depending on a number of contingencies such as age, reason for infertility (including sperm count and health of the sperm), the clinic doing the procedure, and other factors, the success rate was about twelve percent. By comparison, the success rate now for a single cycle of IVF for women under thirty-five is more than thirty percent. (That rate drops precipitously after a woman is over forty.) Currently, there are more than eight million IVF babies. That number is growing quickly as IVF becomes easier, more affordable, and more successful. The demand is also growing as couples are increasingly putting off starting families and nontraditional family structures become more mainstream.

No doubt, though, it was the hysteria accompanying the arrival of the first "test-tube" babies that brought debates over advanced reproductive medicine to the fore. Rothman, who was a professional colleague and personal friend of Steptoe, was in the middle of the maelstrom, if not at the eye of the storm, and would soon partner with Century City Hospital colleagues Mark Surrey (an OB/GYN doctor with a developing specialty in female fertility), Hal Danzer (now a leading reproductive endocrinologist), and Chuck Sims (a pathologist) to open one of the first IVF clinics in the US.

Initially, the media attention on IVF focused on women, the new miracle mothers. This is not surprising, considering the history of women being blamed for infertility even though men are just as likely to be responsible. Nevertheless, before direct-insemination techniques became standard in IVF—and a godsend to previously subfertile men—IVF was a boon to hopeful mothers who had issues with fallopian-tube function or irregular ovulation or just didn't produce enough eggs. IVF also increased the demand for donor sperm as an answer for would-be mothers with subfertile partners and women without male partners who wanted to experience motherhood.

Years after IVF became widespread, it would have a significant impact on subfertile men. Intracytoplasmic sperm injection (ICSI)—the procedure by which a single sperm cell is injected directly into the cytoplasm of an egg—combined with advances in sperm retrieval (many pioneered by Rothman) all but rendered notions of male infertility obsolete; an isolated sperm cell could do the job of conception, opening up baby-making possibilities for couples previously thought to be infertile.

It was the men's side of the equation that Cappy focused on. His talks on male infertility helped to bring an uncomfortable subject out from the shadows, as well as offer remedies for couples who desperately wanted to conceive. The use of donor sperm for conception and sperm banking became a hot topic, in no small part due to Cappy's enthusiastic promotion. "Clinical Aspects of Sperm Banking" may have come out in *The American Journal of Urology* in April 1978, just months before Louise Joy Brown's birth would rock the world, but Cappy's paper, as much as it codified the practice, wasn't the first word on cryopreservation of genetic material—and Louise Joy Brown wasn't even the first so-called test tube baby. For that, we have to go back to the University of Iowa in the American midcentury, when domestic prosperity, modernism, and scientific advances, not to mention a series of serendipitous events, led to the births of the first babies conceived from frozen donor sperm.

The winding path to this event started in 1677, when Dutch tailor-turned-self-taught-scientist Antonie Philips van Leeuwenhoek began studying microbes under microscopic lenses he fashioned himself. Leeuwenhoek, one of the first to widely use microscopes, became known as the father of microbiology.

After spending lots of time looking at microbes in lake water, people's mouths, bee stingers, eel capillaries, and lots of other stuff, Leeuwenhoek, at the urging of his scientific contemporaries, trained his compound microscope onto his own ejaculate. Judging by the letter he wrote to the leading scientific organization of the day, the Royal Society of London, Leeuwenhoek was slightly embarrassed about his startling discovery of teeming, wriggling "animalcules" living in his semen.

He wrote: "If your Lordship should consider that these observations may disgust or scandalize the learned, I earnestly beg your Lordship to regard them as private and to publish or destroy them as your Lordship sees fit."

The stoic Royal Society was not put off by Leeuwenhoek's discoveries and published his observations, sanctifying the first studies of sperm biology and, you could say, laying a foundation, albeit one that would lie dormant for many years, for the field in which Rothman would make his mark centuries later—andrology.[7]

More than a century after Leeuwenhoek got the thumbs-up from the Royal Society, a Jesuit-trained Italian priest by the name of Lazzaro Spallanzani took a keen interest in biology and became the chair of natural history at the University of Pavia. Spallanzani is credited with being the first person to achieve in vitro fertilization. He devised prophylactic wax pants for male frogs that prevented their semen from fertilizing eggs laid by the female frogs. When he removed the so-called pants, he took the fluid collected within them and put it in the tank where the female frogs had laid eggs. Conception took place!

Spallanzani, like many at the time, was loath to credit the wormlike creatures found in semen with their critical role in the reproductive process. He even theorized that sperm were parasites and that seminal fluid was just a catalyst for the egg to start forming. Though he remained a devoted ovist, in 1784 Spallanzani produced a litter of pups by inseminating a bitch with a "donor" dog's fresh sperm.[8]

This opened up a slow-rolling world of possibilities for animal husbandry that eventually led to freezing, storing, and shipping sperm—ushering in the practice, if not quite the business, of sperm banking. Still, it was a slow roll to what we see now.

Around the turn of the twentieth century, Russian (and then Soviet) biologist Ilya Ivanovich Ivanov started experimenting with artificial insemination and cross-hybridization among a variety of domestic farm animals. His Frankenstein-like pet project involved inseminating female chimpanzees with human sperm in an attempt to create a human-ape hybrid—

thankfully, to no avail. Ivanov fared much better in applying artificial-insemination techniques to horse breeding— selecting stallions for superior genetic traits, as he saw them, and developing better methods to gather their prize sperm and extend their life.

Ivanov used artificial-insemination technologies to permit a single stallion to fertilize up to five hundred mares as opposed to the thirty to forty that a productive stallion would fertilize naturally. The benefits to livestock and dairy farmers were obvious, and the use of artificial insemination increased dramatically in the ensuing decades. By the 1940s, artificial insemination was widespread among US dairy farmers due to the ability of prize bulls to produce better milk-producing cows.

Then came the original test-tube babies.

"The Birth of the Sperm Bank," by Northeastern University's Kara W. Swanson, which was published by the Iowa Department of Cultural Affairs' State Historical Society in 2012, is a fascinating account of the converging forces that led to the first babies being born from frozen and stored donor sperm. And whether we like it or not, one of the most dramatic advances in assisted fertility for humans can't be separated from agriculture.

Here's a quick history.

By 1952, up to seventy-five percent of American farmers were using artificial insemination to breed cattle. In the two decades following World War II, milk yield per cow in the US jumped sixty-five percent. What's more, farmers created cooperatives through which they could share prized bull semen. However, the ability to get the best semen to cows that weren't in close proximity to the bull presented some difficulties.[9]

Going back as far as Ivanov, innovations in extending the life of sperm, such as using egg yolk and milk and/or cooling the sperm, had been tested. But what if you could not only extend the life of a prized bull's sperm long enough to get them across the country, but also long enough to use them even after that prized bull was no longer productive.

By 1950, British researchers had found that by using the sweet, nontoxic liquid compound glycerol, they were able to freeze and then thaw fully motile livestock sperm. Frosty, the first calf produced from frozen sperm, was born in 1951. This was such a milestone that one of the project's leading researchers exclaimed, "Time has lost its significance." *The New York Times* reported that death was no longer "a bar to being a father."[10] And this was just a cow.

Universities with strong agricultural departments continued research into protocols for sire selection and for cryopreservation. The democratization of prized-sire semen for improved domestic cattle and livestock production depended on the ability to safely freeze, store, and ship that semen. Efficient use of liquid nitrogen and improved containers made a big difference: Breeders could choose the best sperm from far-flung places...possibly even after the prized bull had passed.

Of course, humans had been experimenting with artificial insemination, too, though it came with a pitched moral and ethical debate from which livestock breeders were more or less exempt. In other words, there wasn't a Pope Pius XII of dairy farmers to brand the procedure "entirely illicit and immoral" as that pope did in 1949.[11]

The Catholic Church, as you might have guessed, had gone on record a century and a half earlier opposing any form of artificial insemination among humans as a separation of sex and conception. It stuck to its guns even as this method of conception grew more common. The first accounts of artificial insemination date to the late eighteenth century, but it was in the 1930s that it became more than whispered about. Kara Swanson, in "The Birth of the Sperm Bank," assigns the credit or blame for coining the often-derogatory term used for assisted contraception to German physician Hermann Rohleder and his 1934 book, *Test Tube Babies*.

According to Swanson, the American Gynecological Society had by then haltingly endorsed artificial insemination as "a useful means of treating infertility." This was a major breakthrough, considering that so long as the man in the equation could achieve an erection and ejaculation, infertility had been widely considered an entirely female issue.

By the mid-1930s, though, as Swanson reports, even *Scientific American* recognized that artificial insemination could be a solution for tens of thousands of married and apparently fertile women who couldn't conceive because their husbands (not stated, but implied) were infertile.

Before long, artificial insemination had produced thousands of babies—along with all the attendant handwringing you might expect from pious quarters. It wasn't just a conundrum for theology, though. Doctors and lawyers fretted about legal and moral implications: Were children born of artificial insemination "legitimate"? What rights and claims did they have on inheritance? Was this adultery by medicine?

Then there were the more esoteric moral questions. What were the consequences of divorcing sex, or even sexuality, from reproduction? Aldous Huxley's *Brave New World* and George Orwell's *1984* both imagined dystopian futures in which artificial insemination was used to maintain biological elites and enforce totalitarianism.

The influence of eugenics, which gained notoriety during the rise of fascism in Europe—especially in Germany—in the 1920s and '30s, didn't help the public perception. Swanson notes that when Lillian Lauricella gave birth to twins after being artificially inseminated with her husband's semen, her doctor, Frances Seymour, enthusiastically discussed applying donor sperm to make eugenic babies. *Scientific American* wrote that the potential use of donor sperm through artificial insemination was "one of the most significant developments in the history of man," and Nobel Prize–winning geneticist Hermann Muller championed selective human breeding.

Maybe Huxley and Orwell were right to sound the alarm. What happens when humans are created like Frosty?

In light of Swanson's definitive account (which was neatly synthesized and recapped in a 2014 *Atlantic* article by Alexis C. Madrigal), it's not surprising, in hindsight, that the answer to that question would come from the University of Iowa in the middle of the Farm Belt. Nearby Iowa State University had one of the most storied agricultural colleges in the country and by midcentury was on animal husbandry's cutting edge, which meant artificial insemination.

Meanwhile, following the formation of the American Society for the Study of Sterility in 1944—the first professional association for treating infertility—the University of Iowa opened its first fertility clinic in 1952. The university was also undergoing vast improvements to the medical hospital at which the fertility clinic was seated. The doctors there were dealing with a large demand for artificial insemination. It didn't take a genius to look at successes in animal husbandry and wonder whether the use of frozen sperm had human applications.

How Dr. Raymond Bunge teamed up with Jerome Sherman, an expert in electron microscopy and tissue sectioning, to produce the first human Frosty is a fascinating story worthy of its own book. In short, Sherman was recruited into the same University of Iowa urology department where Bunge worked. The university hospital had state-of-the-art freeze-dry machinery, and Sherman was hired to freeze-dry and analyze kidney tissue. When reading up on cryopreservation techniques, he'd become interested in sperm and how they could survive at low temperatures.

Sherman learned about the successes in recovering sperm motility with glycerol after freezing and thawing, and, of course, about the successful fertilizations of chicken eggs and cattle using previously frozen sperm. Sherman started practicing on his own sperm, freezing them and looking for the right combination of protocols that would maximize viable sperm after thawing.

He and Bunge eventually met. Bunge, who was looking to make a name for himself, got Sherman's sperm research sanctioned and paid for by his department, with a focus on freezing and thawing sperm for use in the fertility clinic. When Bunge felt he was getting the knack of things, they recruited the clinic's obstetrician-gynecologist, Dr. William Keettel, to perform the inseminations using frozen donor sperm.

This was a bold move, to say the least, given that the pervasive and persuasive voice of religion was adamantly against artificial insemination in those days, and still is for the most part. Of course, fertility doctors who were treating involuntarily childless couples had a much more positive view on the possibilities. Artificial insemination with donor sperm, however, was especially fraught. Even Bunge wasn't immune to considering the potential eugenic applications once Sherman had achieved a sixty to seventy-eight percent survival rate of viable sperm after thawing.

On the brink of their breakthrough, Bunge wrote: "This research has tremendous implications, both philosophical and clinical...the spermatozoa of great men can be preserved for long periods of time and perhaps a race of superior individuals can ultimately be expected."

He was talking about the first sperm bank, which now existed at his fertility clinic, and how it might be applied to a better brand of human. But even as he mused about a superior race, he didn't know if frozen sperm would work in humans.

He had his answer by July 1953, when the clinic had three pregnancies from frozen sperm on its hands. All three pregnancies came to term and resulted in normal births. The April 9, 1954, Sunday edition of the *Cedar Rapids Gazette* greeted the news, not by celebrating the now-realized dreams of the three new mothers, but with the blaring headline "Fatherhood After Death Has Now Been Proved Possible."

The brave new world had been crossed into, and the backlash was significant. Fertility clinics would not turn back from sperm banking, but sperm banks receded quietly into the background after these first "test tube" babies were born.

For a while, anyway.

Chapter 10

We're Going To Need Bigger Tanks

AFTER BUNGE AND SHERMAN helped deliver the first "test tube" babies to the world, the idea of using donor sperm selected and acquired from a sperm bank in order to conceive quickly became as notorious in its time as IVF-conceived babies would almost a quarter-century later. For many, Bunge and Sherman put into question the very concept of conception, which was long considered, especially in religious circles, to be the province of God and good fortune.

In the blowback against scientific meddling in the realm of the sacred, little heed was paid to the often cruel, forced, and unfortunate nature of marriage and conception throughout history. Especially, of course, for women who were commonly viewed as a commodity in transactions of property, power, politics, and bloodlines, yet given little say in the matter. Artificial insemination, though—this was simply going too far for the moralists.

In the wake of the furor, the practice of using frozen sperm selected by a doctor (sometimes even in consultation with the would-be parents) to assist in conception never went away, but it did recede to a somewhat furtive practice among doctors and fertility clinics using mostly anonymous sperm donors. Cappy Rothman was among those to bring sperm banking out of the shadows and into the mainstream. It wasn't an easy sell, though.

The early-twentieth-century mainstreaming of eugenics theories didn't help. Humanists sounding alarms about the selective-breeding potential of sperm banks added their voices to the religious objections. And it's true, sperm banks did bring out some latent interest in the crackpot theories of eugenics. In fact, just as Cappy was starting to promote his sperm bank as a viable alternative for couples with subfertile men—not just an option for patients being treated for testicular cancer or vasectomies to preserve their genetic potential—an eccentric California millionaire exhumed the decades-old eugenics bogeyman.

Robert Klark Graham, who made his fortune in shatterproof eyeglasses and contact lenses, opened the Repository for Germinal Choice in Escondido, California, in 1979, just a year after Rothman published "Clinical Aspects of Sperm Banking." His idea was to create a sperm bank for high achievers, such as Nobel laureates. Graham hoped the bank would help produce "superkids"—the term the hopped-up media coined for the Repository's offspring-in-waiting. The press called it "the Nobel Prize Sperm Bank," and questions about racism and eugenics understandably followed.

The effort did not win favor when physicist William Shockley—the Bell Laboratories research scientist who helped commercialize a new transistor design and, in the process, spawned Silicon Valley—became the first sperm donor. Aside from being a brilliant physicist and electrical engineer, Shockley was also a proponent of white genetic superiority and saw a role for eugenics. Shockley turned out to be a widely reviled figure, but Graham made the mistake of heralding Shockley's contribution of genetic material to the bank as a "superb asset."[12]

The Repository for Germinal Choice never quite recovered from the taint of white supremacist Shockley's frozen sperm deposit. No other Nobel laureates dropped off genetic material at the bank. Graham was forced to lower his standards somewhat.

Still, he insisted his donors and the women who sought their sperm meet certain criteria: They had to be white, married, Mensa-eligible (possessing IQs in the ninety-eighth percentile), and heterosexual. In essence, it remained a commercialized endeavor in elitist genetic engineering and, as such, wasn't the best public face for the nascent sperm-banking business.

Of course, the privileged have long practiced some form of genetic engineering. The democratization of individual agency is a relatively recent—and still not global—idea. That goes for agency in the matter of choosing a partner, too. The powerful have always had leverage when it comes to enhancing their gene pool, even if they haven't always been successful. On this subject, Cappy is reminded of the story about Isadora Duncan and George Bernard Shaw.

As the tale goes, Duncan wrote G. B. Shaw as follows: "My dear Mr. Shaw: I beg to remind you that as you have the greatest brain in the world, and I have the most beautiful body, it is our duty to posterity to have a child." Whereupon Mr. Shaw is said to have replied: "My dear Miss Duncan: I admit that I have the greatest brain in the world and that you have the most beautiful body, but it might happen that our child would have my body and your brain. Therefore, I respectfully decline."

Robert Klark Graham died in 1997, and his superbaby sperm bank shuttered just two years later. Some 218 children were conceived from its donor sperm, and if any of them became a groundbreaking genius, we have yet to hear about it. As it would happen, when Graham was nearing his deathbed, he reached out to Rothman to see if Cappy would take stewardship of his project and tried to sell Rothman on it by claiming that Mensa was onboard with the bank. As a courtesy or out of curiosity, Cappy called Mensa International to check on its affiliation with Graham's sperm bank. Mensa said there was none, and that was the end of that.

For all the misgivings and missteps, though, Graham did usher in a major change in the field of fertility—though not in engineering super sperm. Rather, it was the idea that a woman or infertile couple had choices when it came to donor sperm. Prior to Graham, the clients took whatever their fertility doctors gave them, often with little knowledge about where the sperm came from. Doctors generally tipped their choices in favor of sperm that would likely produce a child that could pass for the couple's at a glance. Over time, though, couples, or at least the women, increasingly wanted to know something about what sperm were available to them.

As a result, sperm banking slowly started becoming a commercial enterprise, as well as a medical practice, and at the crux of this was the concept of choice. With the advances in semen storage and the ability to recover viable sperm after freezing them, along with improvements in insemination techniques and practices, patients were rapidly gaining agency through assisted reproduction. Reproductive medicine was becoming simultaneously more democratic and more commercial. Among the first to openly market and promote a sperm bank—and the quality of the sperm it stored—Cappy Rothman was at the forefront.

Still, he had significant predecessors. The California Cryobank may have been a couple of decades removed from the first sperm bank Raymond Bunge and Jerome Sherman established at the University of Iowa back in the early 1950s, but the line connecting it to the University of Iowa traces back, like so much of this story, to the Tyler Clinic. In 1975, Cappy received a letter from Raymond Bunge inviting him to join the reproductive staff in Iowa. This was twenty-two years after Bunge and Sherman announced their breakthrough in a short paper published in the prestigious British science journal *Nature* in October 1953. The American equivalent, *Science*, had earlier rejected the paper; its editors thought it would be premature without first knowing whether the three pregnancies under discussion succeeded to birth. The short, clinical and passively voiced announcement in *Nature* got to the point without much editorializing: "The ability of a glycerol treated, frozen and thawed human spermatozoon to fertilize and actuate the human ovum has been observed."[13]

The news traveled quickly despite Bunge and Sherman's no-drama announcement. *The New York Times* followed with a news brief, and *Science* asked for a follow-up article. The backlash to the news came quickly, too, inspiring one Iowa state legislator to write the University of Iowa to complain that it was treating humans like animals.

Back to the Tyler Clinic connection. Before the full impact of Sherman and Bunge's breakthrough had completely landed, Ed Tyler—arguably the most prominent fertility specialist on the West Coast—invited Bunge to address the local branch of the American Society for the Study of Sterility. Tyler also asked Bunge to write a more complete report on the three pregnancies derived from thawed donor sperm, to be published in the Society's relatively new journal, *Fertility and Sterility*.

The article, coauthored with Sherman and Dr. William Keettel, the OB/GYN who performed the inseminations, went into greater procedural detail than the one in *Nature*. Even so, as Kara Swanson noted, "Conspicuously absent from this clinical paper, as from all previous papers and from the press announcement, was any indication whether the frozen sperm used to inseminate the women was donor sperm or husband sperm."

Given the prevailing mores, it's not surprising that the source of the sperm was kept under wraps. Remember, again, that the Roman Catholic Church had opposed all manner of artificial impregnation for decades. Even the Archbishop of Canterbury—the head of the Church of England, a breakaway sect started so Henry VIII could more easily dispose of spouses who failed to yield heirs—lobbied in 1948 to make the use of donated human sperm a criminal act.

Consider, too, that around the time of the Iowa experiment, there was still broad concern that only deviants and undesirables (not the undergrad and graduate students who provided most of the genetic material stored in sperm banks) would be sperm donors.[14] In fact, a year after Bunge addressed the American Society for the Study of Infertility, neighboring Minnesota, a progressive state, failed to get legislation off the ground that would have recognized donor insemination as a legitimate means for producing legal heirs. In other words, a child conceived from a donor was consigned to a legal limbo when it came to hereditary rights.

Of course, the pregnancies initiated by Bunge, Sherman, and Keettel progressed regardless of the controversies swirling around them. All three pregnancies resulted in normal newborns. Bunge, though, shrank from the hoopla and public backlash that accompanied their triumph and quickly receded from the public eye.

The University of Iowa's sperm bank continued to operate, and every now and then a baby would be conceived from its frozen sperm, but the procedure was considered experimental for many years to come. Bunge turned his attention back to his initial area of research: urinary cancers. Cappy, preferring to stay in California, did not take Bunge up on his invitation to join the reproductive staff in Iowa. Sherman continued to work in cryobiology and on improving the standards and status of sperm banking. In 1976, Swanson notes, he drafted the first certification standards for freezing and storing human sperm—sperm banks, in other words.

Following the 1978 birth of Louise Joy Brown, the first IVF baby, Bunge's contributions to assisted reproduction got a critical reassessment from the press and his peers. By then, sperm banks had become more commonplace, though they were used more by men undergoing medical treatments such as radiation or vasectomy, or those about to enter military service. Even with the advent of IVF, fresh sperm remained the preferred method for artificial insemination through the seventies.

After leaving the Tyler Clinic, Cappy Rothman continued promoting the benefits of sperm storage for men about to undergo surgical procedures or enter military service, but he was among the first since Bunge and Sherman to recommend donor sperm as a reasonable alternative to adoption for heterosexual couples with male-factor fertility issues. Rothman was ahead of the curve, not so much in offering donor sperm as a viable means for starting a family, but in his willingness to go public. "Sperm banking [donor sperm] seemed to be a good alternative. To most of the guys, even though they didn't like it, it was the only option they had," says Rothman. "It was just offered as an option, and I'd say most of the couples did, in fact, take it, and I started to get very busy."

The California Cryobank began inauspiciously with a single tank in a janitorial office at Century City Hospital next to the office of Chuck Sims, the pathologist with whom Cappy would eventually partner in the enterprise. Steve Broder, a reproductive biologist whom Rothman recruited out of the Tyler Clinic, joined them as a minority partner. Broder would eventually become the cryobiologist and technical director of the California Cryobank. In the late seventies, though, the Cryobank was just a single liquid-nitrogen tank for freezing and storing ampoules of sperm.

"I had it in the janitorial office because I could lock it," recalls Rothman.

Soon enough, a bigger tank was needed, and the operation moved to a radiology suite on the third floor at the Century City Medical Plaza at 2080 Century Park East, where Rothman kept an office. It was here, in 1978, that Rothman had another breakthrough. "I developed the first masturbatorium," Cappy claims. The office where men would produce semen for analysis or donation came complete with four rooms and visual aids. "I plastered the entire wall with erotic pictures," he says.

The California Cryobank's success rate for intracervical insemination (ICI) of donor sperm back in those days was ten to fifteen percent. This is about the same success rate for the procedure today; sixty to seventy percent of women can expect to become pregnant after six ICI cycles. Rothman's down-to-earth, no-shame approach and easygoing, telegenic presence on the scene no doubt accelerated the Cryobank's growth as he increased his public visibility through lectures, via television appearances, and in numerous professional and mainstream publications while speaking of the benefits of frozen donor sperm. "I guess I was articulate enough and good-looking enough that they liked having me on TV, and it was new," says Rothman.

The need for frozen-sperm storage soon outran the weight-bearing capacity of the medical plaza's upper-level floors. In 1979, following the season of the big fire, Rothman and Sims took a big gamble and bought a building on Gayley Avenue in Westwood. "We had to go someplace and be on the first floor, so we bought a building in Westwood, and that was the location of the first sperm bank," says Rothman.

The tanks proved useful for more than sperm. Rothman's expertise in cryopreservation was called upon by plastic surgeons who needed nipples to be preserved after mastectomies, or by surgeons preserving thyroid glands or whatever types of human tissue or cells might need to be kept on ice for a variety of medical purposes. "It was a nice time when you could do things that you thought were going to be helpful and not hurt anybody," recalls Rothman.

Diane Vieira, an upbeat woman who would work at Rothman's side for years, came onboard on April 1, 1979, just as the new operation was getting underway. She'd commemorate her start date every year by jokingly threatening to quit: "April Fool's!" As for the dearth of remedies for subfertile men in those days, Vieira says, "There wasn't much that could be done. You were stepping into experimental stuff. Initially, Cappy and I prepared the sperm for insemination and did inseminations in the office, both ICI (intra cervical insemination) and IUI (intra uterine insemination). Some of the gynecologists were uncomfortable that we did the inseminations. As long as they were referring patients for sperm preparation, they felt that the patient should return to their offices for the insemination procedure." As Diane was moving to Palmdale, coming in on weekends to Century City would be an inconvenience. Referring the patients back to the gynecologists for insemination worked out well. This also gave Cappy more time to focus on andrology. "Cappy would say things like, 'One of these days, they are going to take a single sperm and put it into an egg.' It sounded so sci-fi."

While intracytoplasmic sperm injection was still more than a decade away from supercharging the effectiveness of IVF and opening new markets for donor sperm, donor sperm was quietly taking hold as an option for traditional couples. "It was a whirlwind," says Vieira. "It was so busy—[Cappy] was one of the few who worked in male infertility."

Vieira recalls that Rothman would experiment with time-lapse, polarizing and microscopic imagery captured by attaching 35mm cameras to microscope lenses in order to view the sperm in action and provide patients an up-close-and-personal look at their sperm. In a way, he was bringing their genetic material to life. "We were kind of flying by the seat of our pants," says Vieira. "Cappy had no end to his enthusiasm. He was teaching everybody. He was very open. Anyone who had any interest was invited to watch the practice." As far as embracing avant-garde remedies for reproductive issues, Vieira says, "We had the concept of 'yes.' Cappy was the only person allowed to say 'no.'"

In his new clinic in Westwood, Rothman now had a direct line to patients and clients and didn't have to worry about "stealing" patients from urologists who didn't have fertility services in house. "I was a one-stop shop," he says.

～

IN THE MONTHS AND years after the fire, Cappy threw himself into his career like a man with a new lease on life. By 1979, the sperm bank he started in a janitorial office had a new building and had been incorporated as the California Cryobank. His private andrology practice was taking off as well. In the realm of reproduction, if there was a question about sperm, Cappy became the go-to guy.

The next step seemed obvious, and in 1981, Rothman and a group of Century City doctors, gynecologists, and urologists, including Mark Surrey and Chuck Sims, opened an IVF clinic within Century City Hospital. The Century City Reproductive Center opened less than a year after the first IVF baby was born in the US and was the third IVF clinic in the US. Cappy and his crew were among the first in the country to grasp the far-off future in which we are only now arriving, one in which barriers to conception would all but cease to exist. Cappy invited his friend, Patrick Steptoe, to the opening of the Century City Hospital IVF Clinic. The celebration was held at the Hilton Hotel in Lake Arrowhead. It was Patrick Steptoe and Bob Edwards who helped Elizabeth Brown have the first IVF baby. Following Arrowhead, Mr. Steptoe invited Cappy to tour and be involved in the clinic at Bourne Hall, Cambridge, England. For Cappy, this opportunity was very exciting. Cappy still remembers going to the Pink Geranium, a restaurant that dates back to the mid-seventeenth century and was known as Prince Charles' favorite restaurant, with Steptoe and his wife Sheena.

Just as the IVF clinic was getting started, Rothman was invited to give a lecture at the Meiji University in Japan. The lecture was meant to focus on the growing field of andrology and reproductive medicine, but the trip would prove fruitful in other ways. Rothman, a longtime archery enthusiast and practitioner, was introduced to both the Japanese longbow and *kyūdō*, the Japanese art of archery. This happened when he asked the concierge at his Tokyo hotel to set him up with a martial arts center so he could get in some target practice while abroad. When Cappy arrived for the class, which was on the roof of a downtown building, the *sensei*, a petite but stern woman, handed him a small bow. Cappy, being left-handed, tried to palm the bow with his right hand. When she grabbed it and put it in his left hand, Cappy switched it back. This got him a quick slap on the wrist. "She slaps my hand and says, 'No southpaw!'"

Rothman recalls that everything was highly formal and ceremonial during the class, and nobody spoke English. "I'm the only guy dressed casually, not in the *kyūdō* attire. Everybody else was dressed for the occasion…They must have been, like, 'Hey, this American is coming up…' So, I'm ignored until I hit the target," Cappy says, laughing. "I'm not even permitted to go pull my arrows. As soon as I hit the target, everybody looks at me and says, 'Cappy-san.'"

The experience is telling in that Rothman found, once again, that being ambidextrous enabled him to function successfully (bullseye!) within a highly structured, traditional environment. It's not surprising, either, that he initiated a lifelong dedication to the Zen marital art "*kyūdō*" during this trip. Cappy purchased two Japanese long bows and two incredible handmade quivers with arrows signed by a master of arrows. As for the lecture he delivered to students at the prestigious Meiji University in Tokyo on andrology and reproductive medicine, Cappy stood at the podium and spoke for forty-five minutes while the students nodded politely throughout. During the question-and-answer session, he learned that the students had been given prepared questions, written phonetically, and that they didn't understand a lick of English and had no idea what he was talking about.

Regardless, Cappy was a hit, and some of the students went out for sushi afterward with him. Sometime during the course of events, Rothman met a precocious graduate student by the name of Kazuhiko Kobayashi who was experimenting with computer-assisted micromanipulation to aid with an experiment he was conducting: the subzonal insemination of sperm into mouse ova. In layman's terms, Kobayashi was using a personal computer to guide hydraulic robotic equipment that injected microscopic sperm past the outer wall of the unfertilized egg and into the zona pellucida, the space around the cytoplasmic membrane.

Prior to Kobayashi, such equipment had been designed and primarily used for research into cell physiology. By using micromanipulation, Kobayashi was able to get a seventy percent fertilization rate in his subzonal inseminations of mouse ova. This put wind beneath the wings of the idea that infertile men might one day be able to conceive through the direct injection of a single motile sperm into an egg.

Though that event was still a decade away, Rothman saw the future while he was in Japan in the form of computer-assisted micromanipulation and the other advanced instrumentation being used there, especially compared with the "barbaric" state of the art in US clinics. Rothman returned to the US with Kobayashi in tow and brought the Japanese approach back to the nascent IVF clinic at Century City. This culminated in a paper and video presentation at the Western Section of the American Urological Association (AUA) on computerized micromanipulation.

"Instruments developed in Japan were far better than anything we had in the United States—different instruments for doing micromanipulation. I came back with all that," says Rothman. "So we were the best IVF center because we had interested doctors, and we had the top equipment."

A key member of the team was Kobayashi. Back in the US, with Kobayashi staying at Rothman's house, the team set about modernizing the Century City Hospital clinic, ergonomically and instrumentally. It was a wild bunch, and Rothman was one of the most progressive in a field making breakthroughs seemingly by the minute. It didn't hurt that he and Surrey were among the hospital's top admitting physicians. They used their leverage to press for the type of micro-assisted fertility equipment Kobayashi had been experimenting with.

For a while, subzonal insemination (SUZI)—using micromanipulation to inject sperm into the zona pellucida, a sort of clear, protective ring around the plasma membrane of the egg—

was the highest advancement in IVF, and therefore, in assisted reproduction. With the equipment and techniques Rothman helped bring back from Japan, the Century City IVF clinic gained a reputation as a national leader. "Cappy was instrumental to me in helping keep that IVF laboratory cutting edge," says Dr. David Hill, a renowned embryologist who worked with Rothman and Surrey during the early days of the Century City IVF clinic.

However, ICSI—intracytoplasmic sperm injection, the process by which a single sperm is injected into the cytoplasmic membrane of an oocyte, thereby putting it deeper and more directly into the female genetic material—would soon render SUZI all but obsolete. For all intents and purposes, ICSI took chance out of the insemination equation. And it was discovered by accident.

Dr. Gianpiero Palermo developed ICSI while experimenting with micro-manipulation tools and techniques to improve subzonal inseminations. In 1990, Palermo went to the Centre for Reproductive Medicine at the Vrije Universiteit Brussel (VUB), then under the guidance of Dr. André Van Steirteghem, to work on his PhD. Palermo, like Cappy, Surrey et al., was intrigued by the potential of micromanipulation to improve subzonal insemination (SUZI) success rates.

Soon after he arrived at VUB for his yearlong research appointment, Palermo was able to get sperm under the zona pellucida but still outside the cytoplasmic membrane. He found the fertilization rate for this technique ran as high as 30.9 percent but dropped dramatically when men had dysmorphic and/or lower-quality sperm.

In Palermo's words, "It was while performing SUZI that a single spermatozoon serendipitously penetrated the oolemma and provided the hint that a direct sperm injection would be more efficient. This was perhaps the birth of ICSI."[15]

Palermo performed the first ICSI that resulted in pregnancy in 1991, and the first successful birth from ICSI came in January 1992. Because intracytoplasmic sperm injection needed only one good sperm, barriers to fertility long thought to be hills too high to climb were suddenly surmountable.

Cappy played a huge role in crashing those barriers. His earlier work in postmortem sperm retrieval had proven that viable sperm could be taken from the epididymis, the tube that connects the vas deferens to the testicle. This was thought to be the final hiding place for sperm prior to ejaculation. Eventually, Rothman was able to get motile sperm directly from the testicles.

After Rothman did that, not even congenital vas deferens blockage or scarring from vasectomies or vasovasostomies were disqualifiers for fertility. With the advent of ICSI, male-factor infertility became increasingly surmountable. These days, a man would have to be sterile not to have at least a shot at conceiving, provided he could afford the advanced procedures available.

ICSI is the industry standard for IVF, and in some European countries it is used in nearly one hundred percent of those procedures.[16] Ironically, one of ICSI's pioneers, Dr. Van Steirteghem, has been vocal in recent years about urging restraint. Van Steirteghem is concerned that ICSI is being used even when there is no male-factor infertility or when the cause of infertility is unknown. Conventional IVF, he says, is less invasive for women and also reduces the chances that sperm carrying genetic defects will be used to fertilize an egg.[17]

Some recent studies have also found sperm and fertility issues among boys conceived from ICSI, though that's not necessarily surprising considering ICSI is indicated for male-factor infertility, so there are likely to be genetic links in these cases. Nevertheless, Van Steirteghem has called for "the need to continue and expand other follow-up studies on children conceived by assisted reproductive techniques."[18]

It's hard to imagine a time before the advances in sperm retrieval, cryobanking, IVF, and ICSI pioneered by Rothman and others put conception within just about anyone's reach. We take a lot of this for granted now. According to the Centers for

Disease Control's Fertility Clinic Success Rates Report, there were 284,385 advanced-reproductive-technology (ART) cycles performed at 448 reporting clinics in the United States in 2017, resulting in 78,052 live-born infants. Today, approximately 1.7 percent of all infants born in the United States every year are conceived via advanced/assisted reproductive technology.

Chapter 11
Family Matters

UNDERSTANDABLY, THE 1978 HOME fire impacted all the Rothmans in profound ways. While it may seem like Cappy was able to immerse himself in his burgeoning practice and growing notoriety, those who worked closely with him, such as Dianne Viera, say the aftermath of the fire was difficult and preoccupied Cappy. Beth Rothman says it frightened all of them—especially the two boys. "Fires are nightmares," says Beth. As bad as it was, though, the fire didn't make Beth want to leave California and head back to her East Coast roots.

So, while Cappy began making a name for himself in the world of reproductive medicine, Beth Rothman threw herself into rebuilding their home. Beth and Cappy didn't necessarily want to rebuild on the same property but financially, that's what made the most sense. The land that the house was on was worth more than both the land and house that they bought six months prior. Beth managed the details of the rebuild while the family shuffled through a succession of rented houses in the Pacific Palisades neighborhood. It was a stressful period. Cappy was at work much of the time, and Beth was left managing two boys as well as the rebuilding process. "It's hard to imagine not even owning a spoon or a pillow. After the fire, we had nothing other than family albums and some family heirlooms. When the Red Cross gave us some money to buy essentials, I had no idea where to begin. As for the boys, Cappy had a patient who, knowing we lost our house in a fire, sent boxes of Star Wars toys, sheets, cookie jars, etcetera, that helped make their transition easier."

The aftermath of the fire was painful. The insurance company that held the Rothman's homeowner's policy, something that was put in place six months earlier, was far from user-friendly, nor was the Small Business Administration. Cappy had to hire fire adjusters to deal with the insurance company. After innumerable requests for an SBA loan, something other disaster victims had been given and Cappy and Beth felt entitled to, they were turned down. The man in charge at the SBA kept telling Beth that the loan was coming. At one point, Beth went to Burbank to meet with him and needed to use the restroom. She noticed something written on the packaging for the toilet cover paper: "I'm quick to tell them that they'll get the loan, but I'm sure to turn them down." This was signed by the agent Beth and Cappy were working with. In a weird way, says Beth, "I felt better. I felt all along that there was crazy making going on, and this proved it." In the long run, Cappy and Beth got the loan.

It was on a trip to Lake Tahoe in the summer following the fire that Beth grasped just how stressful the whole thing had been. "I was in Tahoe and something felt different. I realized it was the first time I'd been smiling and laughing since the fire," she says. "I had been functioning as a robot would." Something else happened in Tahoe. "We saw some babies, and that's when I got the desire."

Beth wanted a girl, and sure enough, she was soon pregnant with Kimberly, who would be due in May or June of 1980. When Beth received the phone call from the doctor's office telling her that she was going to have a girl, she was ecstatic. She remembers being so excited that she startled Brett by her enthusiasm. But as the due date neared, she was gripped by a sense of foreboding. "I talked to the baby a lot in the shower. 'Be okay, be okay,' I'd say. There was some kind of feeling that…I don't know. I never had that feeling with other pregnancies, the feeling that I had to reassure the baby and reassure myself that it would be okay…The whole thing was pretty awful."

Beth recounts this as we're sitting at the large, open kitchen Beth recently renovated for the first time since the house was rebuilt after the fire. It's more than forty years after the terrible event, but as Beth speaks, the years collapse and the memories rise.

A little more than a month before Kimberly was due, Beth noticed that the fetus was unusually active. It felt like she was spinning and doing somersaults in utero. "When I came home, I told Cappy the baby was so active and now she must be sleeping from all that activity."

Beth, though, had an apprehension that something was amiss. After Cappy left for work the following morning, she took out his stethoscope and tried to listen for what she wasn't feeling in her womb. "That's when I called him and called the doctor's office and rode to the doctor's office. That's when I found out."

The baby wasn't sleeping. Kimberly had died in the womb. Beth remains haunted by the likelihood that all the activity she felt before picking up Cappy's stethoscope and before calling the doctor was the fetus "maybe suffocating with the umbilical cord around its neck…If I had only known, I was in the medical building at the time. Maybe something could have been done—I don't know."

The doctor moved to induce delivery, but it would take another day. Beth says she knew that Kimberly would be stillborn and the sonogram confirmed it. Worse, the next morning when it came time for the delivery, Cappy wasn't there. When asked if this marked a difficult period in their relationship, Beth insists it didn't. "No, other than I was very disappointed that Cappy wasn't there with me for that delivery. I felt very much alone…I think he had something in the office.

I think there's no greater silence than not hearing a baby cry when it's supposed to." When asked, again, if this period marked a difficult time in their relationship, Beth reflects and says "Yes," adding, "he should have been there. He should have been with me and our baby. I shouldn't have had to go through that alone. I needed Cappy."

The next day, the hospital called and asked about the Rothmans' plans for the body. "We were not prepared for that call," says Beth.

Cappy says the loss was devastating and notes that Kimberly, had she survived, would be forty. "He had his dreams for this baby, too," says Beth. Perhaps because of those dreams, Cappy "didn't want to have anything to do with" the corpse. A young assistant rabbi from their temple, though, insisted that a burial would be a step toward closure. Kimberly was laid to rest in the summer of 1980. Symbolic of the dissonance in their lives, Beth and Cappy had a meeting with their architect the day of the service. "I think I just robotized myself after losing her, just like I did after losing the house," says Beth. "I wanted a baby girl more than anything. It was a traumatic loss."

Beth and Cappy were determined to keep trying in spite of their loss and several miscarriages to follow. "I had an obstetrician who said, 'You're going to reach this goal,'" says Beth. "He really encouraged it."

Their youngest son, Jason, was born the next year. He was born two weeks early and weighed a little over four pounds. Between his low birth weight and the trauma of Kimberly still fresh in Beth's mind, she would hover over Jason for years to come. "Nobody was good enough to take care of that baby," she says.

Jason was born twelve years after Michael and nine after Brett. He was not born into the striving days when Cappy was making his way through medical school, internships, and residencies. Cappy was by then an established entity, a celebrity in the relatively new fields of andrology and assisted reproduction.

In addition to his practice, Rothman's schedule was filled on a weekly basis with presentations at Cedars-Sinai Medical Center, UCLA, UC Berkeley, St. John's Hospital in Santa Monica, and many more locations, where he lectured on the clinical aspects of sperm banking, the physiological aspects of male infertility, recurrent varicoceles, semen analysis, microsurgery, and other topics of interest in his field.

All this was going on while Cappy fought with City Hall and the Fire Department over safety issues and hillside developments in their charred canyon, moved among temporary houses while his own house got rebuilt, dealt with the stillbirth of Kimberly, established one of the first IVF centers on the West Coast, and welcomed a new son. That was the pace of his life in those formative days. That Rothman's signature moment came in the middle of all this personal and professional tumult is telling.

Remember, it was in the spring of 1980, while Cappy and Beth were still expecting the baby girl they were going to name Kimberly, that Cappy got the call from the chief of neurosurgery at UCLA Medical informing him that Senator Alan Cranston's son, Robin, had been in a car accident. Robin was in a persistent vegetative state, and the senator wanted Cappy's help in retrieving the thirty-two-year-old's sperm for possible future grandchildren.

In "A Method for Obtaining Viable Sperm in the Postmortem State," a dryly titled paper that Cappy published in *Fertility and Sterility* in November of 1980, Rothman detailed the new barrier he'd hurdled with the Cranston case: the world's first viable sperm successfully retrieved and stored from a deceased person. After that, not even death had the final word on the possibility of conception. In this case, Cappy Rothman did.

For all the recognition the Cranston breakthrough brought Rothman among his peers, Cappy would not become best known for this—or for his skills with microsurgery, or for his contributions to the developing field of andrology, or even for the critical role he played in the birth of Brandalynn Vernoff, the first baby conceived from the sperm of a deceased father. Rather, Rothman's greatest distinction would be his association with the California Cryobank, the sperm bank he started, with Beth's strong encouragement, upon leaving the Tyler Clinic. During the eighties and nineties, it grew into the world's largest repository of genetic material. "I was the Cryobank," says Rothman. "When people think of me, they think of the California Cryobank. When they think of the California Cryobank, they think of me."

It didn't come without a cost.

~

AFTER BUNGE AND SHERMAN proved the efficacy of sperm banking for human reproduction, interest in the innovation lay dormant for decades. Slowly, in the mid-seventies, the first consumer-oriented sperm banks started to come online. The California Cryobank was certainly among the most unabashed, thanks to Rothman's affable persona and his willingness to publicly promote donor sperm as a viable solution for infertile couples as well as a safeguard for men undergoing certain medical procedures. Even so, throughout the 1970s, about eighty percent of donor inseminations used fresh sperm, which were still considered more reliable, if sometimes less convenient.[19]

In the eighties, though, several factors contributed to a renewed and increased interest in sperm banking. The most significant was the AIDS epidemic. As the medical community began to get a handle on the pathology of AIDS, it became clear that the HIV virus was most readily transmitted through direct contact with blood and semen.

Furthermore, the virus could take up to six months to incubate and show up in screening tests. Thus, quarantining blood for transfers and semen for inseminations became standard operating procedure. Frozen donor sperm had the advantage of being able to be screened and stored with a time stamp. Cappy and Chuck Sims started quarantining sperm for six months prior to releasing it.

Jerome Sherman, in fact, was central to writing and promoting recommendations that doctors use only frozen sperm for inseminations, and he served as an FDA adviser on AIDS and cryobanking from 1988 to 1992.[20]

Another significant factor was the rise in single women who didn't want the lack of a husband or partner to bar them from motherhood. Then there was the increasing cultural acceptance of same-sex couples who wanted to start families. According to the Human Fertility and Embryology Authority, between 2015 and 2016, the number of single women seeking fertility through donor sperm rose fifteen percent, while the number of single women choosing to have IVF increased thirty-five percent between 2014 and 2019.[21]

Since the seventies, men had started to take on (slightly) more responsibility for birth control in the form of vasectomies, while at the same time, male-factor infertility among couples having trouble conceiving was being recognized. Varicoceles—dilated veins in the scrotum that can adversely affect the sperm's morphology (structure and form)—were coming under increasing scrutiny as a possible culprit in fertility issues. Though a definitive relationship between varicoceles and male-factor infertility remains a subject of debate, removing varicoceles gained traction.[22]

All this was happening while Cappy himself was gaining a reputation as the best surgeon in the region for varicocelectomies, vasectomies, and vasovasostomies—not to mention being the go-to guy for issues involving male fertility and sperm. The table was set.

As well positioned as Cappy was by the time sperm banking started to grow, Beth Rothman insists the business opportunities were not what drove him. "There was nothing opportunist; nothing, not even the Cryobank," she says.

"He does not look at it as a business…because his idea is to help people, and he's magnanimous…for instance, he did a vasovasostomy [vasectomy reversal], from everything I've heard, like no one could, a fantastic microsurgeon, and he would bring in any doctor who asked to come in and observe him. He'd give the bank away if he had one."

Beth thought growing the sperm bank was a great idea. "I could see that there was a need for it. If you ask Cappy, he'll say that I promoted the sperm bank, pushed it into existence. I completely thought it was a great idea," she says. "Most people, not all, of course, have that dream of having a child. For him to be able to help them actualize that dream is tremendously gratifying."

Not all was gratifying or problem free when it came to the California Cryobank. In the late eighties, a call came in from a woman who was looking to find her son's heirs. She wanted to divide his estate amongst them. When Rothman, curious as to why her son died, called and asked, she told him that her son died of AIDS. After speaking to the Cryobank's lawyer, Cappy was told to find out how many clients used the donor's sperm and to contact them telling them that they, as well as their donor offspring, needed to be tested. Forty families were contacted, told of the situation, the need to get tested, and the mother's wish to disperse her son's estate to his heirs. Fortunately, besides the trauma of the situation, no one tested positive for AIDS. There was no interest in receiving money from the donor's will. The donor, as it happened, had not been an active donor for years before AIDS was even recognized.

The growth of the California Cryobank and the demand for Cappy's surgical expertise had taken a toll not just on Beth but also the boys, who were beginning to come into their own. Beth says she tried to have a normal family life focused around family dinners, but she'd often watch the clock strike eight p.m. and realize Cappy wasn't going to make it home on time. "He was away a lot," she says, and as a result, the boys acted out a bit in their own ways. "Brett had major authority issues. In fact, he went to a psychologist who said he didn't even have a male figure to identify with." This harkens back to the authority issues that Cappy had growing up.

Beth adds that Brett now idolizes Cappy much as Cappy idolized his father, but that wasn't always the case. Rothman's absences often left the kids wondering where they fit in with Cappy's priorities. "Actually, when Michael and Brett were growing up, I'd say, 'Don't you want to go to their Little League games?'" says Beth "And Cappy would say, 'No, I'm not interested in baseball' And I'd say, 'But it's not about baseball; it's about your kids. Don't you want to see them play?' 'No, not really.'"

The boys would ask Beth why their dad, when he was with them, couldn't be more like the person he was at work: congenial, upbeat, available. "They viewed him as giving way more to those people and putting up with way more from them. The boys would be hurt about it," says Beth.

When the boys would act out, Cappy's default response was to threaten them with military school—the thing he credits with having saved him. Beth, though, wasn't having any of that. "We fought. Cappy would storm off from the dinner table and be furious with me because I wasn't siding with him but I couldn't. I just couldn't... We went to therapy."

Things kind of came to a head when Beth, who was a teacher when she met Cappy, decided to go back to school to pursue a graduate degree in psychology. "When Jason was born, I was, like, thirty-seven or thirty-eight, and I was nearing my fortieth birthday, and that was a big birthday for me... The anticipation of that number is really big, and right before turning forty, I decided I was going back to school. And I went to graduate school."

At the beginning of their relationship, Beth says she was captivated by how much of a fully formed, cosmopolitan man Cappy already was. Now, Beth was starting to think about where she fit into all of this as an individual with her own ideas. She says this didn't go over that well with Cappy. "He was beside himself that I was going to school, that's all I can say. I think he felt threatened. I don't know…that I had this life apart from him? That he didn't know where it was going? He felt abandoned. Anybody he worked with knew that he felt like I left him by going to school," she says.

Beth eventually finished graduate school and passed her boards but with a young child, it was hard to find time to practice psychology. "I did eventually take on too much, and I had to let some of it go," Beth explains. "All of a sudden, 'Oh, I can be an intern, I can be a student, I can be all this at the same time.' No, it didn't work. Jason started acting out at school, and the headmistress started calling me to pick him up. There was no way that I could be in both places at the same time and my call to motherhood prevailed."

These were hard days and hard years, and it wasn't always clear from the inside where Rothman's singular focus was taking his family. Thomas Carlyle's "great man" theory holds that the history of the world is but the biography of great men. But at what cost to the families of great men? "The period with the kids, that was a long period," says Beth. "We fought and didn't agree with each other, and I questioned us because I didn't like who he was as a father, and that's the truth."

It seems fatherhood was more difficult to master than microsurgery, but as he did with medicine, Cappy learned and evolved. "He's very different now. He's much more involved with the kids. He's a softer person now. He became such a good father," says Beth. "I just marvel at him. It's like if Brett's even mad or says something antagonistic to him, Cappy will call him back to say, 'Is there something I did to bother you? And if I did, I'm sorry.' I mean, that's not the man he used to be. It's shocking to me, and beautiful. It's just amazing."

Still, like many women, Beth sometimes wonders what she gave up in service to her partner's growth and success. "I feel bad that I didn't take the direction and stay on the path versus cave in and go back to what's now sort of an old-fashioned mindset—you should be home for dinner with the kids, you should be home for dinner with your husband, that kind of thing. To develop your practice, you have to be out at night. I don't know. It's not resentment toward him. It's more about me, and I haven't figured that out totally."

～

MICHAEL, THE ELDEST SON, now in his early fifties, is a filmmaker living in fabled Topanga Canyon, upstream and uphill from the surfer paradises of Topanga Beach and Malibu. Topanga Canyon has a rich bohemian history dating back to the midcentury. Neil Young used to live near the beach and threw memorable parties attended by beatniks, hippies, surfers, and musicians. Farther up the canyon, Michael has a tastefully elegant hillside home with a detached studio and a couple of surfboards at the ready should the waves align with a pause in his busy schedule.

Handsome and preternaturally cool in a mellow SoCal way, Michael recalls growing up as a rebellious boy in an often stifling environment. He says that, as with Norman Rothman, when Cappy spoke, "You didn't question it, you just did it. You wouldn't even think to question it." And Michael, like Cappy himself, wasn't inclined to submit quietly to authority. "I was prone to asking, 'Why?' And I think his head exploded a little bit," Michael explains. "I grew up with the constant threat of being sent to military school. That was daily."

A sensitive and curious kid with defiance issues, Michael was relational and intuitive in his approach. This was a challenge for his logic and science-based father. "I think I just naturally have more of a place in my heart that just seeks more of an emotional connection than an authoritarian-type of connection. I don't know if my dad was able to do that so much for me, even knowing his intentions were in the right place… It got to a point where no matter what he was saying, I was going to go in the opposite direction," Michael says. "Speaking with your feelings, having a place to share your emotions, that wasn't a common thing back at that time, especially for men."

Like a lot of first sons, Michael was a case study for the siblings who followed. "My middle brother [Brett] learned early on that if he was going to try to stick his nose in it, it was not going to work out well for him. He learned how to keep quiet and how to smile, and it would not touch him. I was the lightning rod."

Michael echoes Beth in suggesting that the most confusing and challenging thing for him and his brother, Brett, was the emotional unavailability of their father compared to how he presented himself in the world. "I always saw him as one person with other people and a different person with me and perhaps Brett. That easygoing, kind of super generous disposition that he has, I don't think that really came across as much to Brett and myself, but it was clear he had it for everyone else."

It's reasonable to think Cappy may have cultivated a degree of detachment in order to navigate his own hectic childhood; a factor that's not lost on his eldest son. "When you think about it, there had to have been many situations in his home growing up that were challenging. He was surrounded by conflict, so how he doesn't have anything negative to say about his path through life is pretty amazing," says Michael.

It's not all that surprising, Michael suggests, that as a coping mechanism, Cappy focused on the glamorous rather than the darker side of his father's legacy. "I think that's what resonates with him. When you think about him as a young kid, and being in Cuba in the heyday, and your dad was a player, and you got a seat at the table, it had to be super exciting and intoxicating as a youth. And that's why a lot of people got involved in the Mafia, at the time anyway. There was a lifestyle element to, it at the high point, anyway, that was intoxicating. But there was the shadow side that was ugly. And luckily for him, maybe he just didn't get to see that part. So, he just sees the glamour."

Cappy's unique medical pursuits also didn't do Michael any favors when it was time to navigate adolescence. "What he did, as interesting as it is for adults, when you're, like, fifteen, sixteen years old, when you tell your friends what your dad does, that he's into male infertility, take a look at these slides he's working on, and it's a guy's penis and balls and sperm, I mean, talk about opening yourself up for a can of humor whooping," Michael laughs. Eventually, Michael would simply explain that his dad was a doctor and leave it at that.

Second son Brett Rothman remembers that he didn't know about Norman "Roughhouse" Rothman's real life until he was in his teens or early twenties. Up until that point, Roughhouse was "just a cool story." Looking back on his formative years, Brett jokes, "I might have a little of him [Roughhouse] in me."

It's easy to joke about such things now that he's a successful medical salesperson living in San Diego with his wife and two kids, ages four and eight; but as an adolescent, Brett says, "I was going nowhere fast."

Brett found his passion in martial arts, competing in jiujitsu and Muay Thai, sometimes referred to as "Thai boxing." These pursuits acted to quell the angry, tough guy self that he felt he sometimes had. Finding a focus for his career proved more of a challenge. He failed out of Santa Monica College before eventually graduating from Western Washington University. His struggles to find his way during adolescence did, however, have some upside: Cappy put him to work at Century City Hospital, where he progressed from cleaning up operating rooms to being a scrub tech and eventually getting into medical sales.

Perhaps more than his other family members, Brett got to see Cappy in action. "I worked with him in the operating room," says Brett. Sometimes Brett would be in the operating room watching Cappy do hours long microsurgeries. "I certainly enjoyed the dynamic and enjoyed working with him, but I knew of his celebrity at a fairly young age."

Brett remembers a defining moment in the mid-nineties when Cappy threw a party in the lobby of Century City Hospital. "It was all the people who had offspring as a result of his intervention, and from that day on, I saw my dad differently. It was when I saw him not just as a celebrity but as a god. These were people who had been told time and time again that they couldn't have children, and they were so grateful. That was a beautiful day."

Youngest son Jason, a lawyer living in Los Angeles who recently welcomed the newest of Cappy and Beth's five grandkids into the family, agrees that Cappy cast a long shadow. "It was a bit of my identity growing up," he says. "In a way, I was the son of Super Sperm, as I called him, with his sperm shirts and the sperm pens. I think even at my high school graduation, one of my teachers, when she met my dad, she said, 'Oh, you're the king of sperm.'"

Jason recalls this anecdote fondly and says that he used his father's celebrity "for the humorous side" when it came up in conversation. "'Oh, my dad is a doctor. What kind of doctor? A penis doctor.'"

Like his brothers, Jason is also athletic, competing in a handful of half marathons every year. That seems to be a consistent thread through the siblings, along with a hard-earned sense of their own identities and places in the world. Whatever struggles they had in their formative years, all have come to an abiding respect for what their father has done with his life.

"I'm nothing but proud and impressed," says Jason. "He will be one of those people who will go down in history. He's done very well for himself and just with his own willpower."

∼

IN 2010, MICHAEL MADE a film about Cappy and Cappy's two younger brothers, Ronnie and Santy, called *Three Brothers*. The brothers hadn't been particularly close as adults. Their paths were varied and rarely intersected after they left home. The film is a sort of reckoning. In it, Ronnie and Santy seem almost shell-shocked by their experiences growing up with Norman "Roughhouse" Rothman. Santy recalls on film how upset he'd get while visiting his father in prison during one of Roughhouse's stints in federal custody. "You always wanted to believe that he shouldn't be there," Santy says.

There's a scene in the film in which Ronnie recounts how he went to visit Norman in prison and got a new green suit and new brown shoes for the occasion. When Roughhouse got a look at his third son, he said, "What are you…a fucking tree, and your shoes aren't shined."

Ronnie, says Michael, was the one who was most traumatized but also had the most to say. "I was most taken with Ronnie," Michael says. "To me, he said that as if he remembered it like it was yesterday. Clearly the impact of that shut him down." Ronnie confides to the camera, "I can't remember one time he said something nice to me."

The film served as Michael's first significant introduction to his uncles and as an exploration of a family legacy that was felt more than it was seen or discussed. Michael says the takeaway was simple: "Time is short, tomorrow is not a given, don't push things off." Santy died six months after the film was made, and Ronnie died in 2018. The brothers may have never been closer as adults than they were during the filming of *Three Brothers*.

Ronnie's wife, Mitzie, was twelve years old when she came into the Rothman circle. She remembers tutoring Cappy in chemistry when she was in high school, and he was working on getting the credits he needed for medical school. "He was a good student," she says.

Even these many years and accomplishments after the fact, Mitzie and Ronnie remained happily surprised at the way Cappy's life turned out. "Ronnie and I were very surprised that he wanted to go into medicine, and we were happy that he found something that he was very passionate about," Mitzie said when reached at her Florida home not long before Ronnie passed. At the time, both Mitzie and Ronnie seemed in good spirits and good health.

As for her husband's father, Mitzie says that Norman "Roughhouse" Rothman wasn't the warm-and-fuzzy type. "He was just a tough guy." Still, she says, being in "Roughhouse" Rothman's circle had its advantages. "It was very nice. We went to very lovely restaurants. All Ronnie had to do was drop my father-in-law's name, and we were up in front for whatever show we were seeing," says Mitzie. "It was good to be related to Normie Rothman."

Before Cappy found medicine, Mitzie says, "He was having a real good time…His picture would be in the newspaper in the gossip page." Mitzie remembers the anatomy homework Cappy would do on dead cats after he discovered his passion for medicine. "He had that cat splayed out for a long time," she says. "My mother-in-law was a real good sport."

Ronnie says that of the three boys, Cappy seemed most enthralled with "Roughhouse" Rothman and his milieu. "We all thought Cappy would follow in our father's footsteps," Ronnie said. "I wouldn't use the word 'relief'; I'd say we were all incredibly proud that he found medicine and succeeded and became a doctor. He was the first doctor in the family."

Ronnie and Mitzie were lifelong teachers, and their two daughters followed suit. Content with their own lives, they have long since dismissed whatever resentments or jealousies they might have harbored about rich and famous Cappy. "I was always a little bit jealous of the older brother. Not excessively so and not anymore. I'm happy with where I am," Ronnie explained. "He was getting all the girls. If there was a car, he had the better car. He took it as an entitlement, being the oldest… Now I see he's done very well. He lives very well. He's earned what he has. It wasn't just given to him, so I respect that."

Says Mitzie, "From my eyes, as an outsider who came into the family and saw Cappy from his youth to the successful person he is now, I'm so proud of him and the growth and his professionalism in his field and his accomplishments in his field. I've known Cappy a lifetime. It's almost like watching someone grow up, and he did it well. We're all very proud of him. He's a successful professional and a good dad and a good brother-in-law. He's a nice guy."

Michael, who took off for the East Coast when he was eighteen to live with Beth's parents and get a break from the family dynamics, appreciates Cappy's evolution as a father and a man. Now he sees a person who isn't hung up on attachments, particularly to his own identity, and a man who has become a welcoming and generous patriarch to a growing family. "I think things have hit a really nice groove now," says Michael. "How you see him is how he is in his totality…Just to see him navigate through life these days without a lot of resistance."

Through his filmmaking, Michael has also developed a deeper appreciation for what Cappy has done in his career. In 2012, Michael started working on a compelling film called *Kids of 5114*, about a friend's grandson who was conceived through donor sperm. The boy found out he had other siblings from the same donor, and the film tracks their search for one another, following them to an eventual meeting/reunion in Taos, New Mexico, and capturing their halting attempts to establish sibling relationships. "All of a sudden, at that moment when I watched these people come together and the bond they had, I got what he [Cappy] did," says Michael. "That was when it really crystallized for me the impact and the emotional magnitude the work he's done is having on people. It just really moved me at that time."

Cappy's mother, Ethel "Eddye" Rothman, died in 2012. When she passed, she had been happily living in a retirement home overlooking the George Washington Bridge in Riverdale, a nice neighborhood in the Bronx, where Eddye was born ninety-seven years prior and had grown up one of four children sharing a two-bedroom apartment. Cappy says his mother was very supportive in his life and endlessly patient, especially with him, even when he was constantly having friends stay the night or putting cats in the freezer that he would later dissect on the kitchen table. "She was so used to my having friends sleep over that she would say, 'If we were getting robbed, I would probably serve the robber breakfast,'" Cappy recalls. "She was very supportive and proud of me for getting into med school. Nobody thought I was going to be a doctor. They thought I was going to be more like my dad." Beth remembers a holiday dinner, shortly after she and Cappy got engaged, in which Cappy sat at the head of the table as if he were king. Following dinner, the family was asked to stay out of the family room while Cappy (the medical student) took his grandfather's blood pressure. "Yes, the family was proud of him!" says Beth.

Despite all that, and despite Cappy's insistence that his mom was "wonderful," Eddye remains something of an enigma. Cappy speaks of her only in the most general terms. As was typical for the times, she suffered what she suffered mostly in silence. Whatever her feelings were about the fractures caused by Norman Rothman's second family with Olga "Queen of the Mambo" Chaviano, Cappy says Eddye kept the children mostly out of it.

Cappy himself never felt compelled to confront the situation. "I think it wasn't unique to my family. I think it was part of the culture of the day, where men had mistresses," says Cappy. "She kind of knew he was involved with another woman and knew he had a son, Jorge [Faustino] with Olga. She kept asking me right up until she developed Alzheimer's if my father had married Olga... She was aware of some things, not everything. What seemed to bother her more than him having a son was whether or not he married Olga. I didn't know then, and I don't know now."

Cappy says his mother was always an ally to him. "She would stick up for me, and sometimes I needed a lot of sticking up for." He remembers Eddye asking him once—he may have been eighteen—whom he would live with if she and Roughhouse got divorced. He said he'd choose to live with his dad. "He was more exciting," explains Cappy. "My mother was more loving, but my dad was so much more exciting to be around. I guess I was more into excitement then."

Chapter 12

His Own Man

NORMAN ROTHMAN DIED IN October 1985, at the age of seventy-one, ten years to the month after his release from the federal penitentiary. Cappy Rothman was twenty-two when Norman Rothman was first sentenced to prison on gunrunning charges in 1961, and he was thirty-seven when Roughhouse made parole in 1975 after being convicted again on federal charges. By this time, Roughhouse had spent a quarter of Cappy's life in lockup.

The prison time didn't do Norman Rothman's health any favors. He had been ill for months before he passed, mostly from infections that followed a surgical procedure on his neck to alleviate some of his cervical pain. Rothman had chronic acne that was most likely accompanied by minor staph infections. The surgery opened up the way for the staph to enter his blood system, resulting in staph meningitis. "It's almost incurable," says Cappy. "So, for the last four months of his life, he was in the hospital with a series of surgeries and antibiotics. He kept smoking and drinking regardless."

Cappy visited his father in the hospital before he died. Whatever ambivalence he may have harbored about Norman is impossible to excavate at this point. Simply put, Cappy doesn't ruminate on his father. For his part, Norman Rothman was by all accounts proud of his doctor son, but different geographies and trajectories played somewhat of a cruel trick on the father and son. Cappy was young and impressionable during Norman Rothman's "glory" days in Havana and Miami Beach. He seems to have internalized a narrative of his father based on the gauzy memories of a wide-eyed boy who was sent off to school at a young age, and from those of a young man who reaped many of the benefits of having a well-connected father and an all-access pass to Miami Beach's late fifties/early sixties glamour. After his experience at Great Lakes, Illinois, Cappy's interests took a dramatic turn that, in many ways, left his past behind.

Cappy does acknowledge that he asked his father who killed Kennedy but maintains this was his father's only response: "I never spoke with anybody about this when I was living, and I'm not going to talk to anybody about it now that I'm dying."

Says Cappy, "Do I think he might have known who killed Kennedy? Maybe. Do I know the relationship with [Jack] Ruby? No, I don't know it…When I was younger, I saw people go in to see Santos Trafficante Jr., and I remember asking, 'Why's everybody kissing his hand?' And people had names like Sharkey, Skin, Jimmy Blue Eyes. It was Damon Runyon and the cast of La Cosa Nostra. But I didn't know what they were; I was ten or twelve years old…I was always okay with it, whatever it was. Even now. I'm not going to find out about Kennedy. I'm not going to find out about Ruby. I'm not gonna find out about Oswald, about what happened."

Norman Rothman did live to see some of the more remarkable milestones in his son's life, including the retrieval of sperm in a postmortem state. Roughhouse, though, didn't live to see that method used in the conception of a child, an event in which his son played a critical role.

IT WASN'T UNTIL 1999 that the first baby, a girl named Brandalynn Verhoff, was born from postmortem sperm. In many respects, this particular reproductive breakthrough was also a Cappy Rothman production. "I was the one who retrieved the sperm from her father at the morgue. I was the one who froze the specimen. I was the one that assisted in the in vitro fertilization that ultimately led to the pregnancy," says Cappy.

Brandalynn Vernoff weighed eight pounds, five ounces when she was born on March 17, 1999, almost four years after her father died. She is just one of tens of thousands who can track their genetic origins back to a vial of sperm at the California Cryobank, but her creation story certainly ranks as one of the most extraordinary. Cappy went to see the new mother and daughter at St. John's Hospital in Los Angeles right before he was scheduled to fly to Panama for a big conference on advances in treating infertility. Talk about good timing.

"I was giving a lecture in Panama, and in Panama the news broke [about Brandalynn], and I became one of the most famous doctors in Panama. I was treated as if I was royalty. I was a celebrity there for a few days," laughs Cappy. "It was a breakthrough."

The news caused a sensation and sparked the sorts of ethical debates that seem to follow every advance in reproductive technologies. In a report in the *Los Angeles Times* that came out ten days after Brandalynn's birth, Alexander M. Capron, then professor of law and medicine and codirector of the Pacific Center for Health Policy and Ethics at USC, asked, "Is it appropriate to consciously bring a child into this world with a dead father?"

That's just one of the many ethical questions such births bring up even today. Most defy easy answers. Considering Capron's question, there are already a significant number of single-parent households in this country that have nothing to do with postmortem conception, regardless of whether the child was consciously brought into that situation. And the outcomes for children raised in single-parent families vary, as they do in households where both parents are present. One could argue that not having a father (or mother) is better than having a bad one.

Cappy has said his primary focus on these rare occasions is to relieve pain and suffering. Some infertility experts and ethicists, though, question whether dealing with grief in such a way could be unhealthy for the mother, and for the child, should one be conceived through postmortem sperm. The risk of transference from mother to child—using the kid to fill the hole left by the departed father—is too great, they argue.

Other issues concern the rights of the deceased. Any way you perform postmortem sperm retrieval—whether stimulating ejaculation through drug-induced spasms or rectal-probe electroejaculation, or by following Cappy's surgical methods— getting sperm from a dead man, is invasive. So is an autopsy.

So, the ethical debates around postmortem sperm retrieval have generally revolved around the issue of consent, either explicit—in the form of an advance directive, a will, prior written consent, or some other form—or inferred or implied. Some ethicists have argued, though, that the wishes of the dead don't really matter, since the dead no longer have interests. This isn't a particularly strong argument, since, generally speaking, when the wishes of the dead are explicit, they almost always take precedence over the wishes of the surviving. One exception is Dr. Albert Barnes, who amassed an outstanding collection of art and explicitly noted in his will that he didn't want his collection to be housed in Philadelphia. Today, the Barnes Foundation is a prominent fixture in Philadelphia in spite of his wishes. Generally, by law and custom, we typically try not to harm, even the dead.

In situations wherein the deceased has considered or planned for the possibility of death and postmortem conception—soldiers and terminal patients often bank sperm—there are fewer debates.[23] In the Netherlands, prior written consent is required, but not in neighboring Belgium, where proxies are given more leeway in deciding the deceased's interests. Highlighting that arbitrary country regulations are very problematic is exposed in the case of Diane Blood versus the United Kingdom. Cappy met Diane and her father when they were appearing on *The Oprah Winfrey Show* in 1995. While Diane's husband was hospitalized with meningitis and in a coma, Diane requested that his sperm be retrieved and stored. Unfortunately, he died, and soon after Diane requested that the UK release the sperm so that she could become pregnant. The UK refused her request and the Blood Family sued the UK health regulatory branch. After a long period of time and great expense, she almost won. The UK agreed to release the sperm to Belgium for an IVF procedure but not allow her to retrieve the sperm in the UK. Diane went to Belgium, had the procedure, which was successful, and returned to the UK to later give birth to a normal boy.

In Israel, implied consent suffices so long as it's the deceased's partner who has petitioned for the posthumous sperm. Even then, the courts may review the request, and the state requires six-month quarantine periods for bereavement, after which only the wife can provide consent. The option isn't available to unmarried persons.[24]

Around the world, how to handle postmortem sperm is an unsettled issue. That's especially true here in the US, where there are no nationwide laws or protocols. Cases are left to states, municipalities, and institutions to decide. A hospital may not allow a postmortem sperm retrieval, for instance, but a morgue might. Cappy once had to have a corpse transferred from a Catholic hospital to the morgue at Century City Hospital to retrieve the sperm. Since most postmortem sperm retrieval requests follow sudden and unforeseen death, this leaves ethics boards at institutions, as well as practitioners, grappling with notions of consent on a case-by-case basis.

Men who are not facing imminent death don't generally think about the future of their sperm. Various studies show that eighty to ninety percent of men who were thinking about the future of their sperm—men dealing with cancer or infertility issues who have banked their genetic material—do consent to postmortem use.[25] Another poll, conducted in 2014, found that seventy percent of spouses said it would be okay for their partner to use their eggs or sperm after death to make a baby.

Bruce Vernoff wasn't thinking about any of this when he died from an accidental overdose of prescription medicines at thirty-five. He and his wife, Gaby, were happily married. Gaby said she and Bruce frequently talked about starting a family and even had a video of Bruce talking about having children with Gaby. Bruce's death left Gaby mourning both her husband and the loss of the family Gaby and Bruce planned to start.

It wasn't just Gaby who was feeling that loss, either. The parents and siblings of Bruce and Gaby had been looking forward to the couple having children. In fact, it was Bruce's sister, Suzy, who brought up the idea of postmortem sperm retrieval after she recalled reading that a person's sperm can stay viable for nearly two days after death. It was Bruce's family who put up the $35,000 it took to get Gaby pregnant with Bruce's sperm via in vitro fertilization and intracytoplasmic sperm injection of the sperm directly into the egg.

Suzy Vernoff's investigations led her to Cappy, and it was some thirty hours after Bruce Vernoff's death—late in this game—that Cappy was at the morgue retrieving Bruce's sperm. The sperm were in poor shape, sluggish, but there were motile specimens available. Cappy froze the viable sperm and stored them for a year and a half before Gaby made her decision to attempt to get pregnant. After several misfires, doctors were down to the last vial of Bruce's sperm that Cappy had stored at the California Cryobank.

Along with Bruce's parents, Gaby consulted Paul Turek, a doctor at the University of California, San Francisco Medical Center, who was and is a friend of Cappy Rothman. Turek had developed enhanced techniques for identifying the most viable sperm. He stayed at Cappy's home while he isolated Bruce's best remaining sperm. They managed to get one in the right place, and Gaby Vernhoff finally became pregnant in June 1998. She delivered Brandalynn Vernoff on March 17, 1999.

"I think about Bruce always," Gaby told *People* magazine several weeks after Brandalynn's birth. "I'm sad he's [Bruce] not here to enjoy our baby." Bruce's father said, "The bottom line is we have a beautiful baby girl who, but for God and science, might never have been."

The happy ending, though, didn't sway all observers. One skeptic was Sherman Silber, a St. Louis–area infertility expert who helped promote the technique of intracytoplasmic sperm injection that led to the fertilization of two of Gaby's eggs, one of which took. "It's perhaps a psychologically unsound way of helping a woman who has suffered a great loss deal with it through denial," he said in the same April 29, 1999, *People* article. "There is the risk that the baby becomes an intentionally manipulated substitute for her lost husband."

Bioethicist Glenn McGee of the University of Pennsylvania's Center for Bioethics had this to say about Brandalynn's birth: "This beautiful little girl does not mean we should open the floodgates. It sets a dangerous precedent to say there can be reproduction without consent." Yet nobody analogizes it to rape.

Though there has been a bit of federal-level interest in establishing some uniform regulations on the issue of life after death, the rarity of cryogenically preserved postmortem sperm ever being used, puts no great urgency on the issue. Since 1980, Cappy has been involved with nearly two hundred postmortem retrievals, and in only a few cases have the sperm been requested for insemination.

"What I'm finding is most of the time it's done to [ease] the immediate grief of a family with a loss," Rothman told writer Jenny Morber in a 2016 article, "Dead Man's Sperm."[26] "I'm not in a position to judge, looking at the different moralities, societal interests," Rothman argues. "I'm a physician and if I can help someone who is in a great deal of pain—and if you lose somebody you're in an awful lot of pain—that's my calling."

As noted, in lieu of uniform regulations, Cappy established his own guidelines. If there was any disharmony among family members, or a lack of support from the medical facility at which the procedure would be conducted, or if the patient had undergone a vasectomy (implied non-consent), Cappy would not do the procedure. If the family was unified about retrieving sperm from a deceased loved one, Cappy says, his first duty was to relieve the suffering where he could. Those outside the family circle, such as ethicists, who object on theoretical grounds, are merely "intellectualizing" the family's real-world concerns, says Rothman.

In a 2011 *Journal of Andrology* article, Rothman elaborated: "I would re-commend to proceed immediately with postmortem sperm retrieval, but [also] to inform the families there may be some objection to its use. Very rarely will the sperm be used, but giving families hope and decreasing pain is always a kind and healing opportunity for a physician…when I receive a phone call from a grieving family in tremendous pain due to the untimely loss of a husband and/or son and who can be comforted and given hope by sperm retrieval, in the spirit of the Hippocratic Oath to decrease pain and suffering, I facilitate their request. Conditions of refusal are based on a family member's opposition or if the deceased had previously had a vasectomy. To date, out of the approximate [180] postmortem requests I've been involved with, only [three] wives wanted to retrieve their husband's sperm [from storage] and [all] had normal children with IVF/ICSI."[27]

Rothman told *People* that he had no ethical qualms when it came to Gaby Vernoff. "The family told me how desperately they wanted to do it," he said, noting that Vernoff was the first to actually use postmortem sperm in the nearly twenty years and dozens of retrievals he'd done since he performed his first in 1980. "Most of the times I [agree to] do it because I can [sense] the pain—the acute loss of the son or husband...This gives them hope."

Upon returning home from that conference in Panama, Rothman discovered his growing reputation had preceded him. Reporters and television crews, including one from ABC's *20/20*, were lying in wait, surrounding his house. Cappy, who had been flying from Panama to Miami and then on to Los Angeles, weaved his way through the media frenzy and had just one request before fielding questions. "I'd like to take a shower," he told the scrum of reporters.

While he was in the shower, the news crews, which had been plugging their powerful lights into his garage and garden outlets, managed to blow all the fuses in his house.

"So, I come out, and I'm addressing them in a towel wrapped around a wet body, saying, 'Will somebody go out and undo some of the bulbs.' I think they had to use some of the neighbors' electricity. But there's an episode on *20/20* of me being interviewed about the first postmortem baby."

Cappy would make many more appearances in magazines, in newspapers, and on television, appearing on *Oprah*, *The Phil Donahue Show* (several times), CBS News, and *60 Minutes*, where he was interviewed by Morley Safer. Rothman was now a star in the exploding field of reproductive medicine. Life could spring from death.

Nearly twenty years lapsed from the time when Cappy Rothman performed the first postmortem sperm retrieval on Senator Cranston's son Robin in 1980 to March 17, 1999, when Brandalynn Vernhoff was born. This was, arguably, the apex of the notoriety Cappy had been accumulating since Cranston and, subsequently, publishing "A Method for Obtaining Viable Sperm in the Postmortem State," which appeared in November 1980 in *Fertility and Sterility*. That paper was, in some ways, Cappy's "Frosty the Cow" moment: a radical leap in accepted practices that put him on the map—similar to how using frozen donor sperm in multiple pregnancies had put Raymond Bunge and Jerome Sherman on the map back in 1953 and '54. Though the ensuing furor sent Bunge into something of a retreat, Rothman was not nearly as camera-shy. In the wake of publishing the paper, Cappy was frequently in the spotlight, speaking on the efficacy and ethics of both sperm banking and, of course, postmortem sperm retrieval.

Rothman appeared in major newspaper and magazine articles and on local television newsmagazine shows such as KTLA's *Hour Magazine*, discussing sperm banking and male infertility. He made several appearances on the 1970s and '80s *The Tom Snyder Show* ("Male Infertility," June 1986; "Current Reproductive Technology and Ethical Implications," August 1989), and was a featured guest on PBS ("Sperm Banking"), along with many appearances on network affiliate stations in Los Angeles and around the country. CNN was just starting to claim a big share of the news audience in those days, and Cappy appeared on *Sonya Live* in October of 1991 to discuss "Current Reproductive Technology." *The Oprah Winfrey Show* booked Rothman in November 1996 to discuss "Postmortem Sperm and Options," which was the subject for his appearance the following month on ABC's *A.M. Live*. Fox Network News booked Cappy in January 1997 for a segment on "Male Infertility and Options."

While "A Method for Obtaining Viable Sperm in a Postmortem State" increased Rothman's profile among his peers nationally and internationally, two major events put him more squarely in the public spotlight. One was that the growing demand for IVF forced the media to finally catch up to the technological advances and consumer interest in assisted reproductive technologies, especially with the advent of ICSI. The conflicts inherent in the medical applications, along with the ethical implications of cryopreservation, heightened by the AIDS crisis and the potential for genetic research on embryos created in vitro, also contributed to the media's interest.

Then, of course, came the birth of Brandalynn Vernhoff, conceived of sperm that Cappy had retrieved from her clinically deceased father. (Cappy also served as a medical adviser for the IVF procedure that produced the ensuing embryo.) Soon after, Cappy appeared on NBC's *The Today Show* for a segment titled "Live Birth From a Dead Man's Sperm" and on ABC's premier news magazine *20/20* for "Miracle Baby—Fatherhood After Death."

If Brandalynn's birth was guaranteed to bring the news vans around to Cappy's Pacific Palisades home, two other preceding events occurred back-to-back and slightly off the radar that also fueled Cappy's rise as the go-to guy to discuss the brave new world of reproductive technologies. One involved the Catholic Church and the other involved the US Congress.

On February 22, 1987, sufficiently alarmed by how many options for reproduction now resided outside of its approved doctrine, the Catholic Church laid down its law on reproductive technologies. The Catholic Church's *Instruction on Respect for Human Life in Its Origin and on the Dignity of Procreation* (known as *Donum Vitae* or *Instruction*) was intended for a wide audience—Catholics, medical practitioners, the healthcare and pharmaceutical industries, and the policy makers, whom one might argue were its primary target. The doctrinal material was meant to throw a wet blanket on the scientific and medical advances the Church argued were devaluing the "divine" nature of procreation.

Donum Vitae contends, "No biologist or doctor can reasonably claim, by virtue of his scientific competence, to be able to decide on people's origin and destiny." It comes out explicitly against IVF and genetic research on embryos and even artificial insemination, except when the donor sperm comes from a husband. In the methods of assisted reproduction, the Church imagines a world of biological and genetic engineering, crossbreeding with animals, and artificial uteruses for gestating human embryos.

The only sanctified conception, according to the Church, is when a husband and wife have sex. *Donum Vitae* contains a lot of words about the deleterious effect that conception by other means will have on the unity and stability of the family.

It holds, "Marriage does not confer upon spouses the right to have a child, but only the right to perform those natural acts which are per se ordered to procreation." The Vatican states that a child has the right "to be the fruit of the specific act of the conjugal love of his parents." Too bad, though, as far as the Church is concerned, if one of the parents is shooting blanks.

It's important to note that *Donum Vitae* came less than ten years after the first successful IVF birth and that the concern around test-tube babies was still pretty extreme. Nonetheless, when the Catholic Church updated its doctrine on assisted fertility and related science and medicine in 2008, it grew even more restrictive. It added prohibitions against most prenatal diagnosis, genetic screening, and other aspects of prenatal care that are considered, by and large, to be standard procedure.

In some ways, the Church's position is understandable. There's a lot of demystifying going on in medicine and science, and the miracle of childbirth looks considerably more mundane under a microscope than it does when considered in esoteric terms, such as the "the fruitful love of God." Conception, some would argue, shouldn't be reduced to a simple transaction between a consumer and a fertility specialist. And while that remains the case for most people, including those seeking advanced reproductive medicine, the *business* of assisted reproduction can sometimes make it appear as if casual baby making is happening in godless fertility clinics around the world.

In real life, though, it's a safer bet that families (traditional and non) and single women who seek the arduous path through IVF or donor insemination consider the fruits of their efforts to be nothing less than divine. By the same token, plenty of families who follow a religious doctrine forbidding even birth control aren't exactly thrilled when the "fruits of marriage" yield an eighth child.

Donum Vitae, nonetheless, argues for legal sanctions against IVF and donor insemination. Even masturbation for the purpose of harvesting a husband's sperm for IVF is flagged as morally illicit because it's "dissociated from the conjugal act, the actions of which are directed to human fertilization," therefore rendering any resulting conception "deprived of its proper perfection."

In 1986, the Ethics Committee of the American Fertility Society (AFS) issued "Ethical Considerations of the New Reproductive Technologies," a report that stood in direct conflict with the Catholic's Church's *Instruction*. The AFS gathered again in 1987, in the spirit of the Church's call for "reflection" on the matter, and again reiterated its fundamental opposition to *Instruction*'s doctrine in a statement published in 1988.

Cappy weighed in on the *Donum Vitae* controversy in a peer-reviewed 1989 article published in the *HEC Forum*—the prestigious publication of the Healthcare Ethics Committee Forum International. *HEC Forum* is geared toward practitioners, healthcare administrators, risk managers, ethicists, social workers, and anyone with stakes in the debate about the rapidly changing field of fertility. In his piece, Rothman liberally references AFS's 1986 report. Even with that institutional safety net underneath him, Rothman's piece is very much his own, a gutsy and highly readable rebuttal of the Church's doctrine.

Citing the Hippocratic Oath, Rothman notes, "The impetus today is to provide a very small population of infertile couples with an opportunity to nurture their own biological child." Medical practice, he writes, "does not easily distinguish between the suffering and illness associated with infertility and the suffering caused by other disease processes."

Rothman points out what many would see as a fundamental flaw in the Vatican's *Instruction*—the notion that there is "good conception and bad conception" and that "good conception" results almost exclusively through intercourse between a married couple. As the AFS notes in its report, the Vatican sanctifies the conjugal act itself and sets aside consideration of a larger view of marriage.

As Rothman put it: "The AFS's ethics committee questions how the Vatican can conclude that the 'fruit of his [or her] parents' love' must, in all circumstances, mean sexual intercourse. Secondly, the Ethics Committee wonders how separating the unitive and procreative individual acts entails a separation of the goods of marriage. Rather, the Ethics Committee sees marriage as involving the *relationship*, not necessarily the conjugal act."

In other words, Rothman and the Ethics Committee argue against a sort of *Handmaid's Tale* view of marriage, contending that intercourse is one of the goods of marriage, but that the goods of marriage involve more than just procreative sex. For instance, having a partner with whom to navigate life. Sometimes, as Rothman points out, that entails confronting fertility issues. In such cases, the partners involved in the relational aspect of the marriage increasingly have choices, and that's a good thing.

The Vatican's doctrine may attempt to point out legitimate questions about our ethical disposition toward the unforeseen consequences of IVF, such as surplus embryos, but instead ends up largely prescribing a wholly limited conception of marriage and partnership. How closer to divine than IVF are those conceptions? And what about the rights of children born of chaotic, strife-filled marriages, or drunken one-night stands?

At the same time Rothman was taking on the Catholic Church, Al Gore tapped him to work with the Congress of the United States' Office of Technology Assessment. The OTA was active between 1972 and 1995 and was conceived as a nonpartisan assembly of experts meant to provide members of Congress and their staffs with unbiased and authoritative analysis of the scientific and technological issues of the day, whether regarding healthcare, climate change, the internet, or advanced reproductive technologies.

Congressman Gore picked Rothman, along with dozens of leaders in the field of fertility and medical ethics, to help formulate a congressional report in the wake of both the Vatican's *Instruction* and the American Fertility Society's "Ethical Considerations of the New Reproductive Technologies" and a subsequent statement in response to the *Donum Vitae*. The OTA report was, in some ways, an arbitration.

Simply titled *Fertility*, the OTA report is a nuanced, sober, and mature assessment, the likes of which we don't see much in these partisan times. (In fact, Newt Gingrich shut down the OTA in 1995 when he was the Republican House leader, basically stating that objective reporting on science was against his party's interests.) It recognizes that rights guaranteed by the Constitution include *liberty rights*—natural rights based on human freedom to pursue happiness so long as it doesn't coerce or injure another person—and *welfare rights*—rights that place demands on others, such as the right to an education. It finds that for fertile couples, the right to produce offspring is a liberty right in that it demands only that others don't interfere. For infertile couples, though, the right to reproduce is a welfare right in that it requires active responses from the community even if the couple can afford to pay.

In his 1989 paper for *HEC Forum*, Rothman points out that the American Fertility Society's ethics report also recognizes that society and most religions in the US generally support fertility enhancement when it comes to fertility drugs or surgical procedures that attempt to repair causes of infertility, and furthermore, that IVF and donor insemination are widely accepted within marriages. He also notes that there is a spectrum of support for insemination involving single parents and issues of embryo storage, cryopreservation, and abandoned embryos.

The OTA report also addresses the different philosophical positions on the "personhood" of embryos. Those vary from what one might call a coldly scientific position that an embryo is simply genetic material that holds no meaning without the attendant goals and aspirations of its producers (in which case it could be available for research or even for sale), to the argument that embryos have transient rights (in which case it's okay to dispose of an embryo on genetic or other grounds but not to use it in commerce or research), to the Catholic Church's position that embryos should be treated as fully developed people with all the unalienable rights we confer on them. Then there's the American Fertility Society's Ethics Committee view that fertilization is "a process, not an event," and its belief that "The degree and nature of respect and moral value accorded to the human pre-embryo rises continuously until birth."

The OTA basically concluded that the major issue government confronts isn't whether certain assisted-fertility practices should be legal or regulated (for instance, there is no law or regulation on what to do with surplus embryos), but whether government should be involved in the welfare rights of infertile couples to reproduce. In other words, rights to reproduce with the help of advanced reproductive methods grow more problematic and lose support when the government is involved in paying for the procedures. The OTA cautions against this.

In his paper, Rothman concludes with the ethical consensus—supported by a Hastings Center analysis of policy statements from eight developed countries including the US, Canada, the UK, Germany, France, Australia, the Netherlands, and Spain—that IVF is and should be medically indicated for infertility and even some issues related to hereditary genetic disease but that the use of clinical IVF for social engineering or eugenics should be discouraged.

Regarding surplus embryos, the OTA report also acknowledged that cryopreservation has some clinical and scientific value: In the future, cells from embryos will likely be used for cellular rejuvenation to provide insight into how mutations happen and to determine the impact environmental factors play in cell development and how organs form. The report suggested that there should be term limits on storage although no consensus had been reached on the length. It recommended that couples be left to determine what becomes of their surplus embryos as long as they are not used for profit or commerce.

There was then, and continues to be, less consensus—even within the fertility field—on what to do about a conflict that started brewing as the use of donor sperm increased throughout the eighties and nineties and has now reached critical mass: sperm donors' rights to privacy versus the rights of their offspring to know their genetic legacies and their extended donor families. It is not surprising that Cappy Rothman, whose California Cryobank would become the world's largest sperm bank, would be at the center of this rising storm.

Chapter 13

The God of Sperm

ONE MORNING, A FEW decades ago, Cappy Rothman woke up in his sleeping bag on top of Half Dome in his beloved Yosemite. Rothman had been making the Half Dome pilgrimage for years to bear witness to the Perseids meteor shower, a summertime astronomical phenomenon that peaks every August 12. "I had an air mattress that I'd blow up, and I had a sleeping bag that was pretty good, and I'd watch the meteors," Rothman explains.

Up there on Half Dome, 4,737 feet above the valley floor, the night sky and the number of stars in it would appear infinite. Looking up at a vast universe illuminated by the twinkling of countless wellsprings of light and the possibilities of life, Cappy couldn't help but draw parallels between what he saw from atop Half Dome and what he saw when he looked at a semen sample under a microscope. A healthy ejaculate contains between forty million and 900 million sperm cells. On a cellular level, that's almost like putting a galaxy under a microscope.

A significant number of those sperm cells can be found at the California Cryobank, which quickly grew from its modest one-tank beginnings in a repurposed janitorial office at Century City Hospital into its own galaxy with many constellations of human life orbiting around it. It is said the Cryobank now has enough genetic material on ice to repopulate the world should we survive a near apocalypse.

At the Cryobank's primary location, a sprawling two-story, two building campus in West Los Angeles at the intersection of La Grange and Armacost avenues, forty large storage tanks are located. More recently, liquid-nitrogen tanks to preserve umbilical-cord blood and stem cells have been added alongside those frozen-sperm storage tanks, not to mention 800 or so cryogenic shipping containers to get the genetic material where it needs to go in its state of suspended animation.

It's a large operation, employing 170 people at six locations nationally. In the middle of the parking lot adjacent to the building used to store the genetic material, a 6,000-gallon storage tank for liquid nitrogen rises into the sky. Nearby is a backup power generator that can keep things subzero cool for six months should the power grid go down. The California Cryobank headquarters has parking for 150 vehicles.

The facility is also home to six tastefully appointed masturbatoriums designed by the longtime head of marketing, who happens to be a woman. Rothman, you will recall, was the first to include such an amenity at his initial sperm bank in the early days after the Tyler Clinic. Back then, he put cutout images from *Playboy* and the like on the wall. The current offerings run the gamut from mild pinup erotica ("For some guys, it doesn't take much," Rothman told the *LA Weekly*) to contemporary digital porn.

Rothman, the *Star Trek* fan, is responsible for much of the facility's overall vibe as well as its particulars. The aesthetic is meant to convey an optimistic vision of a future that is unfolding within its confines. Inside, just past the receptionist, sits a large rectangular room for an additional ten large cryotanks. Each of these tanks contains 20,000 ampoules of sperm, color-coded for ethnicity. Each ampoule holds at least sixty million spermatozoa.

Six oversize paintings occupy much of the wall space above these tanks. The paintings depict Cappy's take on human evolution: the Big Bang, molecules emerging, sperm forming, and embryos developing. Cappy says he likes to be reminded that something as big as life "starts out so small." It's also great marketing. Prospective clients touring the facilities see the miracle of conception and gestation within their grasp and start to realize that the road to birthing a child isn't as long as they might have thought.

There are photos of babies everywhere and a good number of them represent the genetic legacies of the anonymous donors who made their deposits at the Cryobank for $100 to $125 per pop. Much of this sperm bounty is deposited and preserved long before its future customers have any inkling that they will need it.

The Bible may consider masturbation a crime against procreation. At the California Cryobank, it's how families get started. "If you look at my office, you will see many hundreds of pictures, and every Christmas, I get many more baby pictures," says Rothman, "and some of the nicest things, where somebody will say, 'Are you Dr. Rothman?' And I'll say, 'Yep,' and they'll say, 'I want to thank you,' and they'll show me a picture of their child. I mean, this is a better reward than anybody could really get."

A 2007 LA Weekly cover story about Rothman, titled appropriately enough "The God of Sperm," posited that the California Cryobank had enough supercooled sperm on site to repopulate the world several times over, and when you consider that it sends between 30,000 and 34,000 ampoules of sperm around the globe every year, it might seem like that's exactly what it's trying to do.

After the domestic market, Israel—which encourages its soldiers to freeze their sperm before going into the Israeli Defense Forces and has liberal laws for widows seeking to use those sperm—along with Chile and Russia, make up the largest international markets. Every year, California Cryobank sperm are responsible for thousands of pregnancies, domestically and internationally.

Infertile couples initially made up the lion's share of customers, but advances in IVF methods, including ICSI—the process by which a single viable sperm is directly injected into the egg's cytoplasm—have reduced the need to call upon donor sperm in the case of subfertile men. These days, single women and lesbian couples are the biggest consumers of donor sperm. Rothman estimates that the number of souls connected to his sperm bank family tree is approaching seven digits. "On the other hand, I do vasectomies," Cappy jokes. "So, maybe it balances out."

Up at Half Dome, Rothman would think about how Carl Sagan spoke of the stars in the sky. "He was talking about millions and billions of stars, and I'm talking about millions and billions of sperm...how much sperm do we have? Nobody can answer that question. It's got to be a phenomenal number with zeroes going out forever."

On one of those years-ago trips to Half Dome, Cappy arose just as the sun was starting to scale El Capitan's 3,000-foot southern face—the so-called Dawn Wall, just a few miles to the west. The sun was high enough already to make silhouettes out of a group of kids perched on the opposite side of the famous granite formation's bowl. Rothman, a serious amateur photographer, saw an opportunity. "There were about twenty kids, and I crawled across an abyss, because on the top [of Half Dome] there's, like, a curve, and they were on one end and I was on the other, and I said, 'Everybody make a different posture.' They were mostly in shadows, the sun was behind them," Cappy says. "I think it's one of the best pictures I've taken."

The iconic shot has been on display in Cappy's office in West Los Angeles for years. In some ways, it's symbolic of Rothman's enviable ability to be in the moment. Family members and friends frequently mention his almost Zen-like ability to roll with things—sometimes for better and worse, they might add.

"You'd have to be in the flow with him, kind of this Zen thing he was into, or there would be challenges," explains the Cryobank's longtime operations manager, Diane Vieira.

We can rewind a little bit to understand how that Zen-like quality Vieira speaks of came into play at a critical juncture in Rothman's life that had as much to do with the explosive growth of the California Cryobank as anything. As we've noted, in the few years between Cappy leaving the Tyler Clinic and losing his house in the 1978 fire, the ambidextrous Rothman, working primarily out of Century City Hospital, had begun to establish himself as one of the top surgeons in the world for vasectomies, vasectomy reversals, testicular cancer, or any of the many reproductive issues a man might confront. By adopting microsurgical techniques earlier than most of his peers, who would often visit Rothman's surgery to learn from him, Cappy became the fastest gun in the West.

Rothman guesses he did about four thousand vasovasostomies, a surgery that requires a delicate touch, during his time as a surgeon. Most urological surgeons do six a year, but Cappy would do three a week. He would set the tone by cranking music and having a support staff, some of whom were charged with keeping Rothman cool.

"Cappy in his heyday was a real force to be reckoned with," the renowned embryologist David Hill tells me. "Even when he was in his fifties and sixties, he was quite something. He was also one of the best microsurgeons I've ever seen. When he did surgery, he would get so hot under the lights and the robes, that he would ask the surgical assistant to cut up the back of the robes and the scrubs so he could cool off. He sometimes required ice packs to be placed on his back."

Rothman gives some credit to what he describes as his own attention deficit and hyperactivity. When he finds something to focus on, he really focuses on it. "I could do a bilateral vasovasostomy in an hour and a half. It would take most people four hours. I knew the anatomy so well. You could not surprise me about the anatomy, even if you'd had prior surgery. I was compulsive about that," says Rothman. "I loved surgery. The music, the environment...How many people get to do what they like, are good at it, and get paid well for it?"

Several things happened that would force Cappy to focus more on the California Cryobank in the years to come, though not before he left his mark on fertility practices here and around the world. In fact, Rothman's contribution to IVF is often overlooked, even, as earlier mentioned, he started one of California's first fertility clinics with Chuck Sims (who would become Cappy's partner at the Cryobank) along with gynecologist Mark Surrey and reproductive endocrinologist Hal Danzer at Century City Hospital. Rothman was the andrologist on the team—the expert on male fertility—while Surrey and Danzer were the experts on female fertility.

Lest we forget, the IVF clinic's origins and cutting-edge reputation go back to the early eighties, when Rothman helped persuade the hospital to invest in the microscopic equipment he needed to perform better semen analysis. To add to this, he also convinced the hospital to bring in Japanese micromanipulation pioneer Kazuhiko Kobayashi, a student of Professor Ogawa at Meiji University in Tokyo, to make their lab state-of-the-art. When IVF started to gain traction following the birth of Louise Joy Brown in 1978, the next major advance was trying to get viable sperm—fresh or frozen—as close to a woman's egg as possible to increase the chances for penetration and fertilization.

With his postmortem sperm retrievals, Rothman had proven that the epididymis, the small duct behind the testes in which sperm mature before being carried through the vas deferens, and eventually out into the world, could yield viable, motile sperm. The final question was whether the sperm factory itself, the testicle, harbored viable sperm, and that, too, proved to be the case. ICSI and the ability to harvest and store sperm from the testicle itself meant that even major issues with the vas deferens or epididymis were not final roadblocks to fertility. Only complete sterility—not even death—would strictly consign a man to absolute infertility.

"Back then, it was the final frontier," says Hill. "There were naysayers saying it couldn't be done. We were doing it sooner than just about anybody. We were hot stuff, and Cappy was right in there with all of it." These advances, Hill notes, changed career trajectories and lives. More options were becoming more available to more men and women. "[Mark] Surrey used to make a living repairing fallopian tubes, and IVF changed that. Those who saw the future were able to grasp it," Hill says.

Both Rothman and Surrey saw the future and grasped it but in different ways. Surrey, who along with Cappy had been a rising star in the small club of fertility specialists, was also in the orbit of Patrick Steptoe when he and Robert Edwards brought the first IVF baby, Louise Joy Brown, into the world back in 1978. Surrey may have seen that IVF was the future of reproductive medicine, but Rothman was right there with him.

In fact, Surrey, Rothman, and Dr. Luciano Zamboni, a well-known path-ologist who brought electron microscopy to the study of sperm anatomy, flew to Sacramento together in 1980 and then drove to UC Davis, where Zamboni had a friend in the veterinary department. The idea was to test out some of what Surrey had picked up from training with the famed Australian embryologist Alan Trounson at Monash University in Melbourne, Australia, as well as what he gleaned in England while observing Steptoe's groundbreaking work.

Trounson was as crucial in some ways to the evolution of IVF, as was Steptoe.[28] His team at Melbourne's Queen Victoria Hospital produced the world's third IVF baby in 1980. Trounson is responsible for introducing hormonal stimulation into IVF in order to induce the ovulation of multiple eggs—a technique he'd used successfully on sheep in his earlier career as an agricultural scientist. Trounson was also the first to develop multiple embryos in test tubes which allowed the fittest embryos to be chosen for implantation. These techniques helped reduce the margins for error and greatly increased the success rates for IVF and are now standard practice.

Surrey's exposure to cosmopolitan innovations in IVF was no doubt invaluable to the mission, but Cappy brought his own locally-grown expertise to the party. "Cappy had been for many years prior to that an innovative andrologist, always on the cutting edge of male infertility work, and therefore on the cutting edge of fertility work," explains Surrey. "Cappy was one of the initial investigators of epididymal sperm aspiration and ICSI, and that proved to be an important part of our practices."

First, though, came the UC Davis monkey business—literally. There, the group was able to stimulate two baboons and practice endoscopic egg aspiration, a technique they'd use when they opened up the third IVF clinic in the US at Century City Hospital, which Surrey credits Trounson for helping them get up and running. "He sent one of his technicians to help develop a lab. Century City was interested in supporting this," says Surrey. "It was a combination of information from the programs in England and Australia that predated our clinical work here."

Cappy says the clinic was an immediate success. By the mid-eighties, though, the team had decided that the hospital wasn't the right place to grow an IVF-focused fertility clinic. Century City was reluctant to give the practice the institutional support—fiscally, as well as the liability coverage—it needed to expand. Though routine now, in those early days, developing multiple embryos, storing embryos through cryopreservation, and doing stem-cell research on them were almost taboo. Surrey and Hal Danzer took the IVF practice out of the hospital and established a private clinic in Beverly Hills. That practice would evolve into what has been known for a quarter of a century now as the Southern California Reproductive Center, considered one of the most successful fertility practices in the world.

Cappy had the opportunity to join them in the venture but decided against it. "I could have been with Mark, but

I thought that it would not have been in my best interests," says Rothman, who feared that aligning himself so closely with a private clinic specializing in IVF would limit his referrals from the gynecologists and reproductive endocrinologists, who had come to view Cappy as *the* man when it came to the male part of the infertility equation, which involved semen analysis, sperm retrieval, problems with ejaculation, reversing vasectomies, and more. "I had very little competition. I was a one-man shop, nationally and internationally, for men," Rothman explains.

Also, as long as the IVF clinic operated within the hospital, gynecologists were welcome to use the facilities for IVF treatment. If they needed a urologist, an andrologist, or a male-fertility specialist, they would call upon Rothman. Cappy realized they would be less likely to do so for fear their patients would get poached if he practiced within a private IVF clinic.

Rothman also had his own vision of the future, specifically what an andrology clinic tailored to men's tastes would look like—a place with pool tables, sports-talk TV, and cigar rooms, not to mention the requisite masturbatoriums to get those sperm samples up and out. He envisioned an environment in which men could treat everything from substandard sperm to hair loss.

Cappy wanted to call it the Andrology Institute—a testosterone-friendly place to hang out, even if low testosterone was the reason you were there. It would not come to pass, though. Cappy says he got too busy with the sperm bank and his private practice to devote the time and energy to bring his vision to life, but you can see evidence of it in today's male-oriented barbershops and body-sculpting emporiums.

For Rothman, there's no need to wonder about the path not taken. By 2020, the California Cryobank had grown into a business with a current capitalization of around a billion dollars. The explosive growth can be traced to the mid-to-late eighties AIDS crisis. That's when the demand for quarantined sperm (i.e., frozen) rather than fresh, untested sperm, exploded—as did the demand for donor sperm for lesbian couples choosing to start families through IVF. But even those external factors wouldn't have made the difference without the unique partnerships that had developed within the Cryobank itself among its two principals, Cappy Rothman and Chuck Sims, and their junior partner, Steve Broder.

Chuck Sims was the chief of pathology at Century City Hospital while Cappy was working within the urology department and making a name as the best microsurgeon around. Cappy was also freezing and storing sperm for interested vasectomy patients as well as for those facing treatments for testicular cancers and other pathologies that could affect fertility. He'd often call on Chuck's expertise to analyze testicular biopsies, testicular failure, and other issues that could explain why a person wasn't producing sperm.

Sensing that there would be a growing market for donor sperm, around 1977, Rothman decided he wanted to do more with the ad hoc sperm bank he was operating in a small storage room at the hospital. As Sims recalls it, Cappy first tried to get institutional backing. When that didn't come through, he went to see Sims. "He walked into my office without an appointment, and he told me he wanted to start this laboratory," recalls Sims. "As I listened to Cappy talk, I reviewed this in my mind—I was kind of an expert in running clinical laboratories. I told Cappy, I'd help him set it up under the premise that I knew about laboratories and how they worked and should be organized. We agreed to go forward."

Sims says Rothman initially suggested calling the operation Century City Cryogenic Center. Anticipating the expanding horizons for preserving tissue as well as genetic material, however, Sims suggested Cryobank. "I came up with and coined the term Cryobank," he says. "To the best of my knowledge, it had never been used before…We never patented the term. It's actually become a generic term."

When Cappy was practicing at the Tyler Clinic, he met Steve Broder, who was then the lab technician. Cappy invited

Steve to join him as a ten percent partner, and the Southern California Cryobank (later becoming California Cryobank) was born. Broder filled the role of technical director, with Sims running the lab, and Cappy as the primary medical practitioner and the public face of the Cryobank.

Business, initially at least, was not booming, and the Cryobank primarily served as an outlet for the partners' secondary medical interests. Rothman wanted to treat infertility from the perspective of an andrologist, still a barely recognized field, and Sims wanted to run a state-of-the-art lab. It was a slow grow, and Sims recalls total revenues for the first year of operation were somewhere around $10,000. Fresh sperm, which are more motile than frozen donor sperm, were still the primary option for insemination in the early days of the Cryobank. The market for frozen donor sperm, though, was slowly growing, and Sims credits Steve Broder with recognizing its potential, particularly among smaller infertility clinics looking for options when it came to male-factor infertility.

Even though frozen sperm are somewhat less motile after they thaw, one selling point was that frozen sperm widened the net of potential donors beyond who was conveniently available at the critical moment for insemination. It also made anonymity easier—something that was valued then by both the donor and the patient.

Rothman and Sims both say it was really the AIDS epidemic that put sperm banking at the core of the Cryobank's operation. Ahead of the curve in both its cryogenic technology and practices and in its laboratory operations, the Cryobank was well positioned when the epidemic hit to set the standards for safe donor sperm by freezing and quarantining the sperm past the virus' incubation period and then clearing them before use. Safe sperm became Cryobank's hallmark. "We had logarithmic growth," says Sims.

Even with all that, though, the California Cryobank may have never become the largest sperm bank in the world if not for a misfortune that befell Rothman when he was at the prime of his surgical prowess. The turning point came when Rothman was on vacation at the exclusive Deer Valley ski resort in Utah in 1999. He was out to dinner with family and friends when the bread plate came his way. Rothman inexplicably dropped it, even though he thought he had it firmly in hand. It wasn't an accident; it was a malfunction, an intensifying of issues with his left thumb that had been impeding the fine motor skills that had been his forte. "I couldn't even button my shirts. I had to use snaps. I couldn't use a nail clipper," Cappy recalls.

Soon after the trip, Cappy had himself checked out, and the test results showed recurrent median nerve damage in his left thumb. Though not a significant pathology, it presented enough of a liability that Rothman's peers and lawyers advised him to stop doing surgery. "So, I basically stopped doing surgery. I really enjoyed doing surgery, and I really identified with being an excellent surgeon," says Rothman, "but that [the California Cryobank] happened because this happened."

What Rothman means is that if something didn't disrupt his path as a surgeon, the California Cryobank might have always played second fiddle to surgery in his career. But it wasn't just the thumb that conspired to convince Rothman that it was time to shift priorities. Not long before his bread plate incident in Utah, Cappy had been wooing a promising young urologist named Philip Werthman into his private practice, which would become the Center for Male Reproductive Medicine. CMRM focused primarily on male infertility—varicoceles, testiculargrams, biopsies, vasectomy reversals, and semen analysis. It was basically the kind of practice Rothman had long envisioned, only without the pool tables and cigar lounge.

Prior to Cappy's association with Phil Werthman, he had another urologist with a unique interest in infertility and urology entertain joining him. Carol Bennett, under the tutelage of Stephen Seager who developed the technique of electroejaculation, was interested in electroejaculation in order to help men with spinal cord injuries or psychological issues surrounding ejaculation. Although the association never came to pass, Cappy and Stephen Seager became friends and shared the recognition of the advantages of electroejaculation for fertility.

Soon after, Rothman offered Phil Werthman a partnership, but the young doctor was considering a competing offer that would move him to Chicago. Then Oprah intervened. Or more accurately, in April 1998, Rothman went to Chicago for an appearance on *The Oprah Winfrey Show* to discuss postmortem sperm retrieval and came back to sunny Southern California with a good-natured ultimatum for Werthman. "It was snowing there in April. It was cold. I told Phil in jest, 'You want to go to Chicago, go to Chicago! I'm not negotiating anymore.'"

Werthman, a former clinical professor of urology at the University of Southern California, decided to stay in Los Angeles. Werthman started CMRM along with Rothman, who has treated more than 30,000 men in the last four decades since parting ways with Surrey and Danzer to forge his own path. It looks as if it was a good move for Werthman, whose own fame grew right along with CMRM. Werthman has been a consultant to major news sources such as CNN and NBC and performed the first live televised vasectomy-reversal surgery on ABC's reality show *Extreme Makeover*.

In 1999, Rothman realized it was time to pass the baton to Werthman. Not long after Werthman came onboard, Cappy had to take a leave from seeing patients to recover from a surgical procedure to relieve his diverticulitis. When Rothman returned to his practice a couple of months later, a third of his patients had migrated to his new junior associate. In typical Rothman fashion, he accommodated to the change seamlessly.

Since 1992, Rothman and his family have had a home in Port Angeles, Washington, which is located just north of Olympic National Park and just south of Vancouver Island. By Werthman taking over most of the practice, Cappy was able to have more time enjoying Washington and traveling the rest of the world. The Rothmans spend summers in Washington on their sprawling retreat that looks out on the Strait of Juan de Fuca, the San Juan Islands, and Vancouver Island.

Getting back to the practice that was becoming more of Werthman's practice than Cappy's, Rothman realized that the universe may indeed have been trying to tell him something. "It was an easy transition for my patients. They liked Phil, and the office, and the [assistants] liked Phil. Phil was good with patients and competent," says Rothman. "I think some of the things we did were just wonderful."

Rothman sold his practice to Werthman in 2000, closing out the chapter of his life that was focused on being a hotshot microsurgeon and a private practitioner in the field of male infertility. He then turned his full attention to the California Cryobank. Those closest to him say he made the transition with stunning grace. "You want to talk about a guy who is well balanced, emotionally stable—I don't believe how well he took that, having to give up something he loved. I still can't get over that," says Beth Rothman. "Just like he accommodated to selling the Cryobank, he knows how to let go."

Eldest son Michael finds Cappy's ability to adapt remarkable. "He seems to be able to transition so gracefully. He's not hung up on things," says Michael. "My dad seems to find inspiration around the next corner. He just seems very happy. Happy and complete in a lot of ways."

Streamlining his professional pursuits did have advantages that made up for whatever loss of identity comes after you give up something you've been among the best at for thirty-five years. The Cryobank was poised in an innovative, dynamic field to take on new markets in new ways, and being the only guy who was allowed to say "no" was another way of saying that Rothman was inclined to say "yes" more often than not. This would prove to be a profitable disposition when it came to the rapidly changing practices and norms (many of them being made up on the spot) of assisted fertility and donor sperm.

ON A MORE PERSONAL level, though, focusing primarily on the Cryobank meant that Cappy and Beth could put even more time into their love of travel, photography, and art. Evidence of this passion is all around them. Cappy's corner office at the Cryobank is crowded with artifacts and photography documenting his travels and discoveries. His office desk and bookshelves are home to an array of small sculptures that feature men with oversized reproductive anatomy and impish grins. These fertility totems are ubiquitous in most indigenous cultures and were even prevalent throughout the West before shame-centered theologies took hold. "An erection used to be considered a sacred shaft," says Rothman, "but after Christianity, it was deemed a demon rod."

Art and photography collected on his travels also adorn Cappy's home. He's a significant collector of the notorious collagist/environmentalist Peter Beard, as well as David Hockney. In his bedroom are prized longbows from Japan, evidence of Cappy's interest in *kyūdō*, the Zen art of archery. There are photography books on every coffee table, and Rothman has digitally stored thousands of pictures that document his travels. By his own account, Cappy and Beth have traveled to seventy-seven countries. They've trekked extensively in China, visited Southeast Asia several times, gone on safari in Africa and India, been to Europe, Scandinavia, Russia, Thailand, Vietnam, South America, Easter Island, Iceland, and more.

One of Rothman's favorite places is Africa. After traveling to South Africa, Botswana, and Zimbabwe, Cappy and Beth were so enchanted with seeing the animals in their natural habitat, as well as experiencing the culture of the people, that they planned to return eight months later with their family.

"Experiencing Tanzania, the migration, the Ngorongoro Crater with the family was incredible" says Rothman.

Another of Rothman's favorite places is Cambodia. "I liked the architecture," he explains, adding that Angkor Wat—the "capital of temples" and the largest religious complex in the world—is among the most impressive things he's ever seen. It was built by Suryavarman II, the Khmer king of the early twelfth century, and it made Rothman wonder, "How could one person become that powerful?"

As you'd imagine, Cappy has travel stories from far-flung places and others virtually in his back yard. Rothman has twice summited the Sierra Nevada's towering Mt. Whitney, which at 14,505 feet is the tallest mountain in the contiguous US. He was also forced to retreat from summit attempts two other times due to altitude sickness. Fittingly, he's also been to the lowest point in the continental United States: Death Valley.

One summer, while trekking in his beloved Sierras, this time in Yosemite, Rothman had a close encounter with a large bear. He was backpacking and decided to leave his car on the Yosemite Valley floor and hike around the rim of the valley. In order to get to the rim, he hitched a ride with a hippie on a motorcycle. "I swore I'd never get on a motorcycle," Rothman recalls. But this guy was the only option around, so he got a ride to Glacier Point, where he rendezvoused with Beth. They camped at about 7,200 feet on top of Glacier Point, which is about a mile west of Vernal Falls and northeast of Sentinel Dome. This was before backpacking permits were required, yet not before camping at Glacier Point was not allowed. Rothman states that "somehow the two of us felt safer with Glacier Point being close by."

That night, he and Beth, snuggled in their sleeping bags, could hear a bear grunting. "It sounded like someone was blowing up an air mattress; only it wasn't," Beth says. They could also hear a spooked man who was camped less than a hundred yards away picking up his tent and pitching it right next to theirs. According to Rothman, the three of them bonded in their fear. After all, they were novices at backpacking! The next morning, Cappy and Beth started hiking down a narrow and steep trail when Cappy decided it was time to take some photos of the beautiful valley vistas. When he knelt down so Beth could get the camera out of his backpack, Beth noticed a big black bear just down the path from them.

"So, I'm kneeling down, and Beth says, 'There's a bear.' I say, 'Where?' She says, 'Right there—in front of you.' I say, 'Start walking back,' and she says, 'He can go faster than us.'" They retreated up the path until there was a tree hanging over a cliff that they could cling to while making room for the bear, who scampered up the granite face of the mountainside without bothering them.

On another trip, Cappy and Beth flew from the Galapagos Islands to Cusco, Peru, at 11,000 feet in the heart of the Peruvian Andes near Machu Picchu. They were staying at the Hotel Monasterio, a point of local pride. The manager and chef, whom Cappy and Beth had been introduced to in Beverly Hills, cautioned them before arriving in Cusco to avoid a big meal and not to overexert themselves on their first day. When they arrived, a big meal was waiting for them. Despite the warning, Cappy and Beth dined as polite guests would.

After the meal, a guide took them to Sacsayhuamán, which is even higher than Cusco. The following day they went sightseeing, and Beth started to feel the effects of overdoing it in the high altitude. She asked to take a taxi—in the middle of nowhere—to get back to the hotel. "Beth wanted to see a doctor," Cappy explains. "I said, 'Well, I'm a doctor,' and she said, 'No, a real one!'" Cappy recalls, laughing. "I had Diamox, but we forgot to take it," says Cappy.

One of the most colorful traveling tales is from a 2004 safari they took in India to photograph Bengal tigers. "We were on a trail looking for tigers, and there was a sighting elsewhere, so our driver hustled to get there and went the wrong way on a trail, and we had a head-on collision," Rothman relates.

A French couple, occupying the vehicle's middle seats, got thrown forward into the roll bar. "They both had bad, bad gashes in their heads. Blood all over the place," says Cappy. The driver was also cut up but not as badly. Before taking the couple to the nearby clinic, the driver asked if they still wanted to see the Bengal tigers. It was more than surprising that the French couple, the husband of which was a serious nature photographer, said "yes." Everyone got to take their photos with the next stop being the clinic. Before getting there, Rothman field-sutured the injuries with the sutures that the couple came prepared with and told the driver to get them to the nearest facility where the couple could get the urgent treatment they needed. When they arrived at the clinic, Beth told the couple that Cappy was a micro surgeon and that he would help them. Rothman was pleasantly surprised that the operating room was a relatively new facility with good lighting. "So, they brought the instruments out, and I'm sitting there just to help or observe or comfort this French couple, but they called in the doctor, and we were waiting, waiting, waiting," Cappy tells me. It's a beautiful spring morning as we sit on his back patio overlooking the Pacific Ocean while a light breeze rustles the juniper trees. "So I started to clean out the wounds, and then I could feel [the gash], and I'm down to the skull, to the bone. So the periosteum [dense vascular tissue] and all of the layers are cut through. And then, they are in pain, so I get some xylocaine and inject it and numb it, and then they show me the instrument tray, and it's like what you'd use for abdominal surgery—big instruments. I said, 'Do you have anything smaller?' And they said, 'Well, an eye doctor comes by occasionally.'"

Rothman, of course, had experience with ophthalmological instruments, having used them to hone his microsurgery skills back in the day. "I said, 'Let me see his instruments,' and they opened the tray, and I said, 'Perfect.' They were micro-instruments with 6.0 nylon sutures as opposed to 3.0, which is like rope. So I started sewing up the couple, and it's probably now an hour or hour and a half later before the doctor shows up, and the doctor happens to be a gynecologist, and she sees me working and sees some of the reconstruction—which happened to be beautiful, even if I say so myself. So I said, 'Oh, here you are,' and she said, 'I can't do this, let me assist you.'"

In a way, as traumatic as this moment was, it was reminiscent of a 747 jet incident that happened years back in 1971. That was the year the Boeing 747 "Jumbo Jet" had just come online—the new gold standard for air travel. It was also the year Cappy Rothman had finished his internship and was in the early stages of a series of residencies on the West Coast—the first of which was a surgical residency at Harbor General in Torrance, a bedroom community south of Los Angeles. Cappy was on his way to Los Angeles from Miami on a National Airlines 747, with his wife and their year-old son, Michael. A young family flying the friendly skies in the newest, biggest, and best commercial jet in the world! It was a glamorous flight to a glamorous destination with a bright future. What could go wrong?

Somewhere over Texas, the plane hit clear air turbulence, which is when separate air masses collide and the air gets bumpy without providing any clues, such as clouds, that trouble is brewing. The 747 dropped thousands of feet without warning. "People were thrown all over the place," Cappy recalls. "The stewardesses were in the process of serving food, so the food was all over the place, all over people, all over the aisles."

Cappy had his seat belt on, but his son, Michael, who was lying on his lap, went flying up into the air. He suffered a broken nose from hitting the ceiling but luckily was okay, otherwise. The flight attendants were not as lucky, and Cappy recalls that most in the back of the plane, where he was sitting, were incapacitated. "They had something broken, something bruised," says Cappy. "The woman behind me said, 'I feel funny,' and I could see she was developing a big hematoma. One of the stewardesses had a compound fracture...everybody was scared." It was literally one of those times when people shout, "Is there a doctor onboard?"

Cappy went to work stabilizing the stewardess' compound fracture with magazines and gauze. The only first-aid item anyone could find was tannic acid, generally used for fever blisters, cold sores, diaper rash, and other skin irritations. "So, I'm thinking, 'What are you going to do with tannic acid?' I don't know what the hell to do with tannic acid…This is their first-aid kit?"

Cappy, always in tune with the fashion trends of the times, says that he was dressed in a flower-print shirt and bell-bottoms with a big belt buckle, and was sporting long hair and a Fu Manchu mustache. "I was a hippie," he says.

A man, who looked suspiciously like the pilot, came out of the cockpit and approached Cappy while he was on his knees setting the woman's compound fracture. "Are you a doctor?" the man asked. Cappy looked up and down the plane at the chaos and the crying passengers and replied, "Are you a pilot?"

The pilot told Cappy to come to the cockpit when he was finished with the woman. The brass at National Airlines was on the radio and wanted a damage assessment and help determining whether the plane should turn around or head on to the planned destination. Since the plane was already halfway to Los Angeles and Rothman feared that if it returned to Miami, he might never get on a plane again, he suggested venturing on. "I converted the back of the plane into an infirmary," he says. "When we landed, there were many ambulances waiting for us."

Rothman says National Airlines gave him a replica model of "Patricia," named for the jumbo jet they were on, and "upgraded me a few times." More than that, the experience was another reminder of why Rothman was initially attracted to being a doctor—the almost superhero-like ability to help people in tough situations. To be the right person at the right time.

Getting back to the safari accident with the French couple that got injured, it, too, encapsulates all the reasons why Cappy went into medicine. "I loved the ability to do that," Rothman explains. "They were so happy, and they continued their trip. When they went back to France, they did not even have to see a plastic surgeon...I remember that as much as I remember seeing the Bengal tigers...I was a hero, and I was written up in the paper." For years, Cappy would receive photos of the couple showing off the work he had done—no scars. Also, the woman proudly wears a locket with the sutures in it as a memento of the experience.

Chapter 14

The Final Frontier?

WHEN CAPPY ROTHMAN FIRST started storing sperm at his makeshift sperm bank after leaving the Tyler Clinic back in 1975, he had two or three regular donors. If a doctor treating an infertile couple with male-factor infertility needed donor sperm, he would call up Cappy. The way it worked was that Cappy and the physician attending to the infertile couple, often a gynecologist in those days, would talk and settle on the most appropriate donor sperm. Among the top criteria was whether the child could pass for the husband's own. It was generally agreed upon that the origin of the sperm used to conceive the child, and the story of the conception itself, would be enveloped in anonymity, if not quite mystery.

Initially, there wasn't a lot of donor variety to choose from, and there were even fewer best practices in place. The use of donor sperm was a somewhat furtive and mostly unregulated area of assisted fertility. Cappy, though, says he was doing more than most to keep standards high. "At least we took the time to work up donors, to make sure they were healthy and that there was no evidence of infection," says Rothman of those early days. "But the other guys probably wouldn't even look at [the sperm samples]. And you had that doctor in Virginia who was using his own sperm."

Rothman is referring to Cecil Jacobson, a fertility doctor who was convicted of fifty-two counts of fraud in 1992 for crimes committed while running a fertility center in Fairfax, Virginia. In the eighties, Jacobson impregnated at least fifteen women (and is suspected of impregnating dozens more) with his own sperm. The women thought they were getting screened, anonymous donor sperm through the center's donor program. No such program existed. In one case, a patient whom Jacobson impregnated thought she was using her husband's sperm. Jacobson's story is sensational but illustrates how cloistered the world of conception intervention remained until relatively recently.

In one case, though, a patient actually wanted Cappy to use his own sperm. Beth remembers the story well because the request came after a rare social invitation the Rothman's accepted from a patient. "Cappy made a point of not socializing with patients," recalls Beth. "So, I was surprised when he told me he wanted to go out with a patient and his wife. Apparently he had gotten to know this couple and the wife kept pushing to go out to dinner with us."

The couples met in Beverly Hills and Beth and the other woman walked ahead of Cappy and the male patient. It didn't take long for the woman to bring up her proposition. Before approaching Cappy, she wanted to know how Beth felt about the God of Sperm donating his own to the cause.

Beth was taken aback. "At first, all I could think about was, forget Cappy, how would I feel about it," says Beth. "Maybe it's selfish, but I didn't want my husband's child as part of their family. I didn't want a tie that would last forever. Recapturing my composure, I answered that Cappy couldn't be their donor, that it was flattering that they wanted him to be, but, ethically, he couldn't."

Fortunately, the couple conceived on their last attempt before opting for a sperm donor.

Nowadays, sperm banking is a big business and there are plenty of donors to choose from, though companies such as the California Cryobank rely on business models that still operate in a relative wilderness when it comes to oversight in the cryopreservation of genetic material, including stem-cell blood and tissue. In these burgeoning biotech sectors, regulation is often ad hoc and handled locally.

The sperm bank that Cappy kept in the janitorial closet as part of his growing andrology practice took its first steps toward becoming as much of a business as a service when Rothman and his partner, Chuck Sims, officially incorporated the California Cryobank in 1977. It would take years before the word-of-mouth, doctor-to-doctor service took on the trappings of a business, one Cappy insists grew organically out of the services he was providing. "If you have a successful service, you will have a successful business," says Rothman.

There is something almost like resignation in his voice when Rothman says this, some recognition that the more successful the business became, the more its business imperatives started to swallow those of the service from which it grew.

The California Cryobank had certainly grown into a big, lucrative business—one that has rewarded Rothman well for his efforts. But in the process, it has perhaps left him wondering just a bit about what he has wrought. "I'm the only one in a company of 230 people who really understands semen analysis," says Rothman, which is ironic considering semen is the goose that laid the golden egg here. "I'm the only andrologist, and I'm thinking, if I were to spend that much money on a company based on science, I would want to have in-depth science. The MBAs are looking at EBITA [earnings before interest, taxes, and amortization], not semen analysis."

By 2014, the California Cryobank had offices around the country (three locations in Los Angeles alone) and business around the world. Its customers, either in the form of user-end consumers purchasing sperm directly from the bank or doctors referring patients, touched every corner of the globe.

By then, though, the business wasn't just about sperm. The "MBAs" Rothman is referring to are the series of venture capitalists and investment groups that first came to Rothman with an offer he had trouble refusing—$90 million for eighty percent of the California Cryobank, plus Cappy and Sims keep the CCB's high-value real-estate holdings while renting space to the new owners.

In a press release announcing the 2014 purchase of the California Cryobank, Longitude Venture Partners II, LP (which describes itself as a Menlo Park–based private investment firm focusing on "venture growth investments in leading healthcare companies"), along with NovaQuest Pharma Opportunities Fund III, LP ("an independent investment firm which manages product and company investments in the global healthcare industry"), address the Cryobank's allure:

California Cryobank has built a strong, global presence in both fertility and cellular therapy, two of the most important and fastest-growing areas in healthcare…the CCB's Stem Cell Division is one of the most active stem-cell banking systems in the world…since 1997, CCB has provided stem-cell services through its FamilyCord subsidiary, including both cord-blood and cord-tissue banking. CCB operates throughout the United States as well as Europe, South America and Asia.

It's the second part—cellular therapy—that is the real lure for these sorts of healthcare "venture-growth" investment firms. The MBAs have compounded the California Cryobank's valuation by multitudes since purchasing it by bundling and packaging it with other asset-rich biomedical companies for other investment firms—kind of like scooping up real estate in an up-and-coming market. The investment firms are in turn betting on being able to commodify the coming miracles of stem-cell therapy and medicine.

In this model, the sperm-banking part of the operation is sort of like the retail end of the business. It keeps the cash flowing. In fact, at the time of the 2014 sale, sixty-five percent of the California Cryobank's roughly $50 million in annual revenues came from donor-sperm sales; twenty percent was from stem cell processing and storage; and five percent from the andrology lab (semen analysis). The remaining revenues derived from egg storage and other client services such as genetic consultations and providing information about donors to their offspring— information that grows more expensive the more in-depth it goes.

It's a business model based on the commodification of reproductive materials, and Chuck Sims, for his part, has some concerns. "I think we embraced regulations early and showed how to work with them rather than fight them. Our company value is in responding to the needs of our clients, and we were successful if we helped them find what they needed and didn't try to sell them on what they didn't need," says Sims. "There are forces that push for commodification that we have to fight. We have to fight it morally, ethically, legally, and organizationally."

Sims, who is no longer on the board of directors of the California Cryobank, worries that the investment groups that own it are more concerned with "trying to flip this" like a real estate company would a property than with its core values. "We are dealing with the lives of donors, siblings, parents. That's not something we should take lightly. I think if we don't take that seriously, it will destroy the values on which the company is built."

Further complicating matters is the fact that the still-lucrative sperm bank part of the operation is becoming increasingly fraught with more challenging market conditions and renewed ethical scrutiny thanks to online ancestry and genetic-tracking sites. Being in a volume business presents challenges when the supply chain gets disrupted, and now that the offspring of anonymous donors are seeking answers to their genetic lineage, such disruption does loom.

For instance, Cappy and the California Cryobank have long been fond of saying that it's harder to get into Harvard Law School than it is to become a CCB donor. True to that sentiment, on its web page, the sperm bank's marketing language is similar to that of a military recruitment center: "Do you have what it takes to become a California Cryobank sperm donor?" And in some regards, the claim about being more selective than the Ivy League schools is true. Not every Harvard applicant will be at least 5' 8", and Harvard wouldn't likely admit that its most sought-after recruits are 6 feet tall, blond-haired, and blue-eyed—the preferred sperm donor. "Danes are what people want," Rothman told the LA Weekly, "so we opened a branch in Copenhagen." In reality, nowadays, people place more importance on the donor's education than whether or not he has blond hair and blue eyes.

While consumers may lean toward some murky form of eugenics after all, even looking like a Dane isn't enough to meet the CCB's standards. Aside from the donor being physically healthy and being enrolled in or having graduated from college, his sperm must pass a rigorous test. First of all, they must be plentiful—200 million per milliliter. (Normal sperm count is somewhere between 20 million and 150 million.) They also must be more than sixty percent motile (good swimmers!), which is more than double the baseline for fertile sperm. Plus, they have to meet morphology standards—look like they are supposed to look.

That's not the end of it, though. It costs the California Cryobank about $5,000 to $6,000 to complete a prospective donor's workup, which includes the application, genetic testing, basic physical and personality tests, testimonials, and other things that go into maintaining a high-standard donor profile that will appeal to discerning patients. The CCB now advertises that donors can make up to $1,500 per month from their sperm, about $150 a pop, a rate increase that reflects the added value sperm donors now have in a marketplace that can no longer offer what used to be the bedrock of the business—anonymity. In other words, it's getting complicated. These days, to make its investment in top-notch donors worth it, the Cryobank needs at least ten to twenty patients per donor.

The controversies around donor anonymity, which had been building for years, appeared to have reached some sort of critical mass just after Rothman sold the Cryobank. The ethics and policy questions about anonymity and the rights of donor offspring to know their genetic history, have recently become a media focus. At writing, there are eight pieces from major publications (*The New York Times, The Guardian, Los Angeles Times, The Atlantic,* and *Los Angeles magazine* among them) with headlines varying on themes such as "Finding the Lost Generation of Sperm Donors" and "An Identity at Loose Ends." Rothman may have gotten out just ahead of a coming regulatory wave. Time will tell.

That's just the tip of the iceberg. A cursory Google search will reveal dozens more such articles detailing the changing mores around sperm banking. The California Cryobank plays a starring or supporting role in most of these pieces. As the largest (or second largest, depending on whom you ask) sperm bank in the world, it has the longest genetic reach. The articles follow a familiar arc. The offspring of a sperm donor from back when anonymity was the standard, discovers that he or she has an unexplored or unknown genetic lineage and wants to know more.

Or, more likely these days, someone conceived of donor sperm sends a DNA swab into 23andme.com or Ancestry. com and finds out he or she has siblings—sometimes lots of them, as we can see in the *Future People: Family of Donor 5114* documentary. *The New York Times Magazine* dedicated an entire issue in June 2019 to a sibling group that had connected through the Donor Sibling Registry, a website set up to connect donor offspring to their genetic fathers and extended families. The piece presented a narrative of excitement, turning into indifference, and then even to dismay, as the number of siblings grew into the dozens. One subject wondered what it meant to be one of fifty siblings. As the news of new siblings kept pouring in, the subjects started feeling lost in the crowd.

Other pieces explored the ramifications of being the off-spring of an anonymous donor—what pieces of identity, both genealogically and psychologically, are left in limbo. Initially, sperm banks were loath to provide identifying information about their donors for fear that doing so would dampen their ability to attract the best possible donors, most of whom were thinking about college pizza money and not their many-limbed family trees when they jerked off into a cup at the sperm bank.

"It's causing a lot of social changes. We have to be very careful with the way we deal with it now. How do you deal with an issue you've never dealt with before? When I started the sperm bank, we used to send samples to doctors, and doctors inseminated patients, and we never knew what happened," says Rothman. "We were just helping them get pregnant. It was just a generous service, where a woman who could not get pregnant could now have a family using donor sperm. At the time, most couples chose not to tell anyone how their child was conceived. To further ensure the secret was kept, the couple went to one doctor to perform the insemination, and once pregnant, another doctor for the delivery. The obstetrician was not told that donor sperm was used, and the doctor who did the insemination did not know whether or not his patient became pregnant. Now, with 23andMe and Ancestry.com, most offspring are told that donor sperm was used and donors are informed that there is no anonymity."

Rothman makes a cameo appearance toward the end of author Dani Shapiro's best-selling 2019 memoir, *Inheritance*. The book, which came out at the beginning of the year, likely inspired the spate of newspaper and magazine articles that followed in its wake and tapped its narrative vein: that identity is a lifelong quest, and secrets told at the point of origin are hard to keep—especially in the information age.

Shapiro, who learns late in life that she's the product of a heretofore anonymous sperm donor from a now-defunct East Coast fertility practice, visits the California Cryobank, hoping for some sort of transcendent encounter with the so-called God of Sperm. She recounts how during her visit, she'd "noticed" the childhood photos, multigenerational family histories, and audio recordings of the potential donors that could be purchased a la carte by those considering donor-sperm options.

She asks Rothman how many potential "souls" are bottled up in the thousands of ampoules full of sperm cells stored in liquid-nitrogen tanks awaiting their fate. Maybe taking a little poetic license, Shapiro notes that to her it seemed as if Rothman had never pondered that question until she posed it.

"Millions, I guess…Millions of souls," Rothman answers.

Shapiro is hopeful that Rothman's recognition that the ampoules of sperm contain potential "souls" will lead to some greater introspection about the meaning of life and how an enterprise based on the ready supply and quick distribution of "potential souls" relates to that. She tells Rothman how it was for her to grow up trying to internalize an identity that never seemed to fit. In the book, the encounter goes like this:

"It can be very traumatic," I said. "To not know. And then find out."

"Why is it traumatic?" Rothman looked puzzled. "You're here, aren't you?"[29]

Shapiro tries to explain what it feels like to find out the father who raised you and whom you "adored" isn't your father and that "the ancestors who supplied your narrative and your identity weren't in fact yours."

"I can see how that would be difficult," Cappy responds in Shapiro's telling. "But you look fantastic for fifty-four…you got good genes."

If this encounter is illustrative of anything, it may be this: Cappy Rothman is interested in life—souls are somebody else's business. But if Rothman seems somewhat immune to the existential questions being raised by business models like the Cryobank's, he gets that the Cryobank is responsible for a "significant population"—many of whom don't know a whole lot about their genetic legacy. Initially, Rothman recognizes that we didn't focus on the ramifications of anonymity, and we were just assisting couples become families. The potential ramifications of sperm banking weren't realized until years later when the donor children became aware of the circumstances surrounding their conception. This came about through sources like 23andMe, Ancestry.com, and the Internet. Dani Shapiro's experience is most likely common to many.

What to do about it is less certain. In countries that did away with sperm-donor anonymity, Britain for instance, sperm banks dried up, prompting some of the nation's citizens to join a wave of "reproductive tourism." Here in the US, there is no coherent regulation, but the industry has responded to market pressures by reforming practices.

The California Cryobank no longer guarantees anonymity to its donors. Instead, it offers a menu of choices such as "open-donor" sperm—meaning the donor commits to one form of contact with his offspring. The contact is facilitated by CCB after the offspring turns eighteen (and is less likely to have legal claims). The contact may be by letter, email, phone call, or some such that provides a child born of donor sperm with some answers about his or her genetic heritage. It doesn't provide for an ongoing relationship with the donor. For a little more, customers can choose "ID disclosure" donors—these donors are known to the recipients upon purchase, and who agree to release their identity to the offspring after a child has reached the age of eighteen.

The CCB also offers a number of items such as Level I: Sneak Peek, which is free and provides clients with a donor's medical history, his personal essay, and the highly subjective "staff impressions." Level II: The Essentials is a $145, ninety-day subscription that gives customers Level I information, plus extended donor profiles, childhood photos, and access to something called "Express Yourself," wherein the donor has taken a blank piece of paper and used it to "present who he is in any form that suits his personality." Level III: Full Access is also a ninety-day subscription that provides all the above along with "facial-features reports, donor conversations, Keirsey reports [a form of personality profile], and Keirsey Q&As for all donors." A prospective buyer can upgrade levels during the course of any subscription.

It's weird stuff and can come off as an upsell ploy to get would-be customers to buy into a manufactured sense of intimacy in what is ultimately a highly transactional process. Then again, it's worth remembering there are millions and millions of children conceived "naturally" who, for one reason or another, have no relationship with one or both of their parents but are doing just fine.

Rothman was originally opposed to "open donors," believing that the Cryobank would have a difficult time getting donors who wanted their identity released. He didn't look at the psychological issues that could arise for the children born of donor sperm. His position has changed. Part of this is due to the eight-year study conducted by his son Michael that culminated in the feature-length documentary *Future People: The Family of Donor 5114*. Michael's film, albeit informative, explores the *emotional* impact of being a child of donor sperm. Similar to adoption, these kids struggle to know their identity, and part of knowing who they are, is connecting with their donor. For many of them, not all, this is the missing piece.

Another aspect of sperm banking that hasn't been appreciated is what it's like for the donor to meet or make contact with his progeny. Mike Rubino, a good looking man, as well as a successful artist, donated sperm for a period of a year between 1994 and 1995. He has twenty-four children and has met twenty-one of them. He has no natural children of his own. Before 23andMe and Ancestry.com were available, connections between donors and their offspring came from clues within the donor's profile or The Donor Sibling Registry, which is a search engine that facilitates identifying the donor with his recipients. Even though recipients were required to sign a document confirming that they would not search for the identity of the donor until their offspring reach the age of eighteen, this contract did not preclude the offspring from searching on their own. When speaking to Mike, it is easy to realize the joy and fulfillment that he has gotten by getting to know his offspring. He proudly tells you that he is now a grandfather of twins! One of the teenage offspring, Jake, from the age of seven until now, lives with him. Most of the women who used Mike's sperm are single or lesbian couples. He seems to have a good relationship with the mothers, as well as offspring. Mike has recently received an invitation, along with six donor siblings, to one of his offspring's weddings.

At this writing, the Cryobank has more than 500 active anonymous donors, 116 open donors, and 134 ID-disclosure donors. In all cases, if a relationship of any kind is to be pursued, it must stem from the offspring and will be mediated through the sperm bank. Meanwhile, the sperm bank is still growing. "We're selling more vials than we did last year, and I think most of it to single women and lesbian couples," says Rothman. "Maybe not most of it, but that's where the growth came."

Donors may still be the moneymakers, but they are not why NovaQuest Pharma Opportunities Fund III, LP, was willing to offer $100 million to Rothman and his partners for the California Cryobank. That money was a bet on a future in which disease, therapy, infertility, and possibly even tissue regeneration are addressed through the cryopreservation of embryos, eggs, and the stem cells they produce, along with stem cells from umbilical-cord blood, all stored at places such as the California Cryobank.

Stem-cell storage promises the possibilities of fighting leukemia and other cancers, of regenerative medicine and of treating immunity disorders. Umbilical-cord fluid is easier to harvest and more potent than bone-marrow fluid, which also has stem cells. For those who can afford it, storing stem cells is marketed as a sort of rainy-day insurance policy for future disease. The capital in these bioengineering investment funds is pooling around a future in which those who can afford to do so will pay well to protect themselves and their children. The new owners of the California Cryobank, now part of CooperSurgical, Inc., is betting that reproductive cells, tissue, and cord blood become valuable commodities.

The science is still very much undecided on how effective or applicable stem-cell therapy or genetic-engineering research on embryos will be in real life. As always, the ethicists have their concerns. As always, some of them will be as unfounded as the howls that greeted Louise Joy Brown when she arrived on planet Earth. Other concerns, such as the ability for those with resources (in this case genetic material) to thrive while those without resources struggle, are likely as real as they've ever been. What isn't uncertain is that all this brave new world stuff is lucrative. Since Cappy sold it in 2014, the California Cryobank has turned over three times to newer and bigger investors. It is now valued at about $1.2 billion and promises to be a leader in the bold biomedical future. Whether that future is *Mad Max* or *Star Trek* remains to be seen. It's a safe bet that Cappy Rothman is leaning toward *Star Trek*.

As for Cappy himself, where does he boldly go now that he's no longer, in practical terms, the God of Sperm? This is one of the few questions that gives him pause and sends him looking back to his childhood for answers.

"I no longer have the same motivations. I don't have to make any more money," says Cappy. "You're kind of motivated to be successful. I have been successful. I've completed that passage, so I'm thinking, what is my next direction to be successful?

"Then, I remember the state of mind I had when I was twelve or thirteen, walking on the Florida beach barefoot. Opening up coconuts, drinking the milk. There was just a certain state of mind. No direction, just enjoying where I was at that time. I wasn't very ambitious. I was just very happy where I was. I'm trying to achieve that."

"The older you get, the faster you get old."

Endnotes

1. T.J. English, *Havana Nocturne: How the Mob Owned Cuba. . .and Then Lost it to the Revolution* (New York: William Morrow, 2009).

2. Jack Colhoun, Gangsterismo: The United States, Cuba and the Mafia, 1933–1966 (New York: William Morrow, 2013).

3. https://www.webmd.com/men/features/vasectomy-risks-benefits#2/

4. https://www.vox.com/science-and-health/2018/9/17/17841518/low-sperm-count-semen-male-fertility/

5. https://www.latimes.com/local/obituaries/la-me-ray-watt8-2009jul08-story.html/

6. https://www.theguardian.com/society/2013/jul/12/story-ivf-five-million-babies/

7. https://www.smithsonianmag.com/science-nature/scientists-finally-unravel-mysteries-sperm-180963578/. Also R. H. Foote, Department of Animal Science, Cornell University, "The History of Artificial Insemination: Selected Notes and Notables," *Jour-nal of Animal Science* 80 (2002), https://www.asas.org/docs/default-source/midwest/mw2020/publications/footehist.pdf?sfvrsn=59da6c07_0.

8. https://www.atlasobscura.com/articles/frog-pants-reproduction-experiment/

9. Foote.

10. Kara W. Swanson (of Northeastern University), "The Birth of the Sperm Bank," The Annals of Iowa 71 (2012), 241-276, https://doi.org/10.17077/0003-4827.1645.

11. Swanson.

12. https://www.nytimes.com/2005/07/01/arts/the-genius-factory-the-curious-history-of-the-nobel-prize-sperm-bank.html/

13. Swanson.

14. Swanson. Also https://www.nytimes.com/2019/06/26/magazine/sperm-donor-questions.html/

15. Andrology 4 (2016), 757–760. Also https://www.vierafertility.com/blog/the-history-of-icsi/

16. https://www.sciencedaily.com/releases/2016/10/161006101459.htm/

17. https://www.bionews.org.uk/page_92197/

18. https://www.sciencedaily.com/releases/2016/10/161006101459.htm/
19. Swanson.
20. Swanson.
21. Louise Donovan, "Why I Became a Single Mom Using a Sperm Donor at Age 37," Elle, April 30, 2019, https://www.elle.com/uk/life-and-culture/a27249263/single-mum-sperm-donor/ .
22. https://www.ncbi.nlm.nih.gov/pmc/articles/PMC2658802/
23. https://mosaicscience.com/story/post-mortem-sperm-donation/
24. http://onlinelibrary.wiley.com/doi/10.2164/jandrol.110.010926/full; https://academic.oup.com/humrep/article/15/4/739/706402/
25. https://mosaicscience.com/story/post-mortem-sperm-donation/
26. https://mosaicscience.com/story/post-mortem-sperm-donation/
27. https://onlinelibrary.wiley.com/doi/full/10.2164/jandrol.110.010926/
28. https://cosmosmagazine.com/biology/alan-trounson-right-side-history/
29. Dani Shapiro, *Inheritance: A Memoir of Genealogy, Paternity, and Love* (New York: Alfred A. Knopf, 2019).

JOE DONNELLY is an award-winning journalist, writer, and editor. He is currently Visiting Assistant Professor of English and Journalism at Whittier College and the editor of *Red Canary Magazine*.